The Parents' Guide to Raising Multi-literate Children

70+ fun, engaging, and purposeful activities to liven up literacy learning.

Yoshito Darmon-Shimamori

The Library 4 Multilinguals

This book is dedicated to
my sons Youjin and Sejin
who are my daily inspiration!

THE PARENTS' GUIDE TO RAISING MULTI-LITERATE CHILDREN

Front cover design: Yoshito Darmon-Shimamori

ISBN: 978-1-914469-00-8 (paperback); 978-1-914469-01-5 (E-book)

First Edition: April 2021

Table of Contents

Acknowledgements

Writing a book might have one author's name, but it is far from being a solo journey! Here, I would like to thank all the people who made this possible.

First and foremost, I would like to thank my wife who has supported me from the beginning and helped me carve out the time to write this book to share my message and support other bilingual and multilingual families. I have also learnt tremendously from her regarding the emotional side of raising children. A lot of what I am sharing in this book regarding this aspect is directly derived from these lessons!

Secondly, I would like to thank my amazing beta-readers who helped me level-up the quality of this book through their thoughts, questions, and reflections. (They are named in alphabetical order)

Amelia Sevilla Martin is a Spanish and French teacher in an international school in Singapore. She has worked across K-12 grade levels, teaching all language levels, including heritage/native students. Amelia is also trained in supporting children with dyslexia and learning difficulties. Little did I know that she offered to beta-read this book while pregnant with her second child, and fighting with morning sickness! (Sorry!) Her professional eye has been very helpful!

I have connected online with Amy González a long time before the first word of this book was even written. Her wealth of knowledge when it comes to resources is incredible! She is a blogger and a mum raising her daughters trilingually, and has, on top of beta-reading my book, tested some activities with her daughters. Can a beta-reader be any more involved than that?!

Josie O'Brien is a researcher, author, and mum of three pre-teens and teens. Her knowledge about dyslexia has been precious to understand how doable the games presented in this book could be for children with dyslexia. It was very important for me to compile games and activities that could be enjoyed by most children. And I am happy to announce that almost all the activities are!

Shawn Fan is a former teacher in Dual Immersion Schools (Mandarin Chinese and English). Her knowledge of Chinese, Bilingual Education, and her teaching expertise made our conversations insightful and full of ideas!! The thought she put into each activity, especially to see if they could be applicable to the Chinese language, have been so precious!

Dr Ute Limacher-Riebold is a researcher, coach, consultant, and author specialising in multilingual parenting and intercultural communication. She is also a polyglot raising her children, now teenagers, with four languages. Her personal and professional insight and advice have been of immense help when it came to clarifying my message.

I feel grateful for all the help they have provided me!

All the ideas I share in this book come to me naturally. But this is due to three people.

My mum, Reiko Shimamori, former researcher specialising in Japanese grammar, who has nurtured in me my curiosity and reflection about the way bilingual and multilingual children learn their home language differently to monolingual ones, as well as how a language translates a culture into words.

My two wonderful university tutors Dr Colin Christie and Marian Carty who taught me, more than a decade ago, how to make language learning fun, and how to take advantage of the here and now to teach languages.

Word from the author

First of all, I would like to thank you for picking up this book. It is the fruit of my personal and professional experiences as well as observations and lessons I have learnt along the way.

I was born and raised bilingual French-Japanese. Growing up in France, I have learnt to read and write Japanese, in France. This has not been plain sailing mainly for one reason, common to many children of bilingual and multilingual families: I was taught Japanese as it was taught to Japanese children living in Japan. Most of my teachers did not realise the barriers to learning that my peers and myself were facing. (I mention them in chapter 1 in the section titled *Barriers to learning to read and write in the home language*).

I have had the privilege of learning to teach foreign languages using the University of Cumbria Approach. It focuses on making the learning and practice of the language learnt purposeful, engaging, and relevant to students. I have since had ten years of experience teaching French, Spanish, and Japanese at various proficiency levels, and I can honestly say that you can teach any language by following a few principles and techniques (detailed in chapters 1 and 2).

In this book, I am sharing my thought processes as well as the pedagogical value of each activity so that when you choose one that can appeal to your child, you know exactly why you are choosing it, and you can therefore ensure the best learning takes place.

Teaching my sons to read and write in French and Korean (respectively, my language and my wife's) with the games I have listed in this book have brought us closer together, and I hope it provides you the same positive experience.

For more resources, please check www.library4multilinguals.com. And to follow our multilingual journey, check my Instagram account **@multilingual_dad**.

The aim of this parents' guide

Verbal communication is a skill acquired naturally at a young age. On the other hand, reading and writing are very much learnt skills. By definition, the process can be much more tedious. Generally, our children are taught how to read and write in the community language in school by **trained and experienced professionals**. On the other hand, the daunting task of teaching these skills in the home languages is left to us parents! The task might very much seem overwhelming and unattainable. This book, therefore, aims to give you all the tools you need to successfully teach your child to read and write in their home language(s) while creating wonderful moments along the way.

You can choose to teach your child to read and write in your home language before, at the same time, or after they have learnt it in school. This parents' guide aims to show you how you can leverage the fantastic job your child's teacher is doing (or has done) to teach them how the sounds that make up the words in the school language are transcribed on paper. (For more details, please make sure you read the section *It's all about LEVERAGE* in chapter 1). Please note that the activities presented in this guide have been devised for children aged 7 and above, who would therefore be familiar with at least one writing system. If you are planning to teach your child to read in their home language before they learn it in school, *The Toolbox for Multilingual Families* (2020) by Ana Elisa Miranda and Dr Ute Limacher-Riebold would be a book to start with. Indeed, it contains a section dedicated to familiarising your child with letters and words before starting to read and write.

The principles and activities displayed in this book can be applied to a variety of languages. Different writing systems contain different difficulties. To address them, this guide will provide examples in English, French, Japanese, and Korean. In chapter 2, based on the examples of Japanese and Korean, you will discover how you can leverage your child's knowledge in the school language to introduce a different script.

This book has been designed to tackle three main worries parents have:

"I am not a teacher. How can I make sure I teach my child properly?"

In *chapter 2 "How to start"*, you will find a detailed explanation on how to start teaching your child to read and write in the home language (with a similar script, or a different one).

Each activity contains a section detailing its pedagogical value so that you can pick and choose the perfect activities depending on your child's needs, proficiency, and tastes. You will also find possible variations to make the activities more accessible or challenging to suit their ability and progress.

On www.library4multilinguals.com you will find teaching tips in video format as well as resources to assist you on this journey.

To make this guide easily understandable to everyone, technical terms have been kept to a minimum. Those used are explained at the back in a *Glossary*. Please also note, occasionally, the sounds of some words have been transcribed using the International Phonetic Alphabet (IPA). Each sound mentioned is listed with examples in the section *International Phonetic Alphabet (IPA)* at the back of the book.

"I have already tried teaching my child but it is impacting our relationship negatively"

You have a parent-child relationship well established, as opposed to a teacher-student one. By trying to wear the teacher's hat you may face resistance. The resulting negative emotions could even tarnish your relationship. Note that in a school setting, a child knows that they are in the classroom to learn and would comply much more easily than if you gave the same task at home where it might just be perceived as extra work.

To help you wear the teacher's hat as well as the parent's one, this book is offering 70+ games and fun activities full of educational benefits. In your child's eyes, however, they will be perceived primarily as fun moments spent with you. Their reading and writing skills will simply develop as a consequence.

"My child isn't as enthusiastic as they used to be"

It often happens that children are very eager when learning the very basics of reading and writing. But as it gets more difficult and the progress is not as fast as they would wish, the initial enthusiasm wears out.

This is why this guide contains more than 30 activities that will help your child practise reading and writing at a letter/character or single word level. The variety will give you choice and will hopefully keep your child excited to discover new games. This guide will accompany you and your child on their progress by offering variations to each activity, and this up to a level where they can read and write confidently short texts.

The importance of being literate for a bi/multilingual child

Being able to speak and understand two or more languages is already a tremendous advantage professionally and personally. Here are a few well-known advantages:

- **Cognitive abilities**[1]: better attention and task-switching capacities, better adaptability to change, less cognitive decline.
- **Open-mindedness and tolerance**: being familiar with two cultures, children grow up knowing that "normal" is subjective and are consequently more tolerant to differences.
- **Better ability to learn foreign languages**[2].

For a child, all the languages they speak enable the expansion of their world by being able to communicate and connect with more people, and by having access to more resources. Learning to read and write will multiply all those

[1] Marian, V. and Shook, A. (2012). The Cognitive Benefit of Being Bilingual. Accessed August 28th 2020 through https://www.dana.org/article/the-cognitive-benefits-of-being-bilingual/

[2] Teber, K. (2017). If Your Child is Bilingual, Learning Additional Languages Later Might be Easier. Accessed August 28th 2020 through https://gumc.georgetown.edu/news-release/does_being_bilingual_help_your_brain_learn_additional_languages/#

benefits. By being able to read, write, and communicate verbally, your child will not always need to rely on you. Teaching your child to read and write in the home languages is gifting them with the tools that will enable them to explore **independently** whatever interest and passion they have!

Consequently, their command of the home language will improve without you always having to be there.

The time you are now willing to take to teach your child to read and write in their home languages is an investment in their future!

Gamifying the learning process

You have surely noticed that your child likes certain activities more than others. And because they are interested, they keep doing it again and again, and consequently become increasingly better at it. No matter the number of failures, your child keeps going without being discouraged in the slightest. This is because they are self-motivated, they find it fun and interesting and want to do it all the time! And generally speaking, we encourage them to pursue their talents. But is "talent" not hours of practice that perfected an interest?

Unfortunately, when it comes to literacy, it is most often considered non-negotiable. And depending on our own experience, we might even think and tell our child: "I know it's not fun, but you have to do it/there is no other way, you have to stick with it". That might be understandable when referring to the community language, but when it comes to the home language, this might not appear as acceptable anymore.

In his inspiring Ted talk titled *The Super Mario Effect – Tricking Your Brain into Learning More*, Mark Rober[3] explains how the way you present a learning experience can change everything. Games create in the learner an inner desire to persevere that is stronger than the natural feeling of wanting to quit after a failure. It puts the learner in a state where they are learning from but not focusing on the failures.

---

[3] Rober, M. (2018). The Super Mario Effect – Tricking Your Brain into Learning More. Accessed August 28th 2020 through https://www.youtube.com/watch?v=9vJRopau0g0

The aim of each activity included in this book is therefore to ignite this inner desire to persevere so that your child wants to keep going and stay positive when facing little challenges. (Please make sure to read the section *Common Teaching Mistakes* in chapter 1.)

Before diving headfirst into different activities, please read the first chapter *Before Starting*. That will give you an idea of potential barriers as well as teaching mistakes to avoid. Then, feel free to go to any relevant section, in the order you want, and to pick and choose activities that interest you and your child.

The activities have been grouped into three sections in chapter 3:

I) Single letters or words.

II) Reading and writing short sentences in a purposeful way.

III) Reading and writing short text.

CHAPTER 1 – Before Starting

In order to teach a child to read and write in your home language(s), there is a lot more than matching the lesson or activity to your child's level. Having the right mindset and environment are crucial, and this chapter is here to help you start your journey on the right foot.

I) Barriers to learning to read and write in the home language

Community language VS home language

The language status

The community language is all around you. In school, the park, anywhere you go, everybody seems to speak that language, and everything is written in it too! At home, you might not speak the community language and have many books and other resources in the home language, but from your child's point of view the community language is likely to endorse a higher status than the home language.

Learning to read and write in a home language is therefore very different from learning to do so in the community language. It was already difficult to learn to read and write in the community/school language, why would your child want to go through the pain again?!

The solution? – Make sure you spend a lot of quality time with your child speaking in your language. The more your child enjoys the time they spend with you, the more your language (their language too!) will become important to them.

Then learning to read and write will become more compelling. Focus on the **quality** over the quantity!

Opportunities to practise

It has to be noted that generally speaking, once children learn to read and write in the community language, they get to practise virtually all the time! They can read the back of the cereal box while having breakfast, the different adverts and instructions on the bus or train, etc. And if we add all the time they spend in school reading in the community/school language, it is clear that your child has fewer opportunities to practise the home language.

The solution? – Make the reading and writing experiences **purposeful** and **motivating**! Give them a reason to **want to** go through the struggle!! (That is what this book is for!!)

II) Common teaching mistakes to avoid

"Let's do a little test to see how much you can remember."

Do you feel the stress going up, and the fear of failing that this sentence provokes? Do not test until success is guaranteed!

There is a common misunderstanding about what "testing" is. A test is generally understood as a label put on the person's ability, a final judgement. Although to some people it can be, it is just one type of "testing" called "summative assessment". Other forms of testing are more generally referred to by the general public as "checking for understanding" (or "formative assessment" as it is called in the teaching jargon).

- You can check the prior knowledge before teaching something new.
- You can check the learning taking place to know if you can carry on or if you need to reinforce / go back on something more basic.

Leave "testing" until the end, and make sure that success is guaranteed. It has to be stressed here that a "test" does not need to be done on paper with a binary "correct / incorrect" outcome. When it comes to reading and writing, it can simply be a game, a book you read together, or a little message you help your child write. By witnessing the stumble blocks, you will understand what your child still needs to work on.

If from time to time you want to formally test your child, remember that you are not testing to trick your child or to include more complex things. You want to use it as a reward and a positive moment so that your child knows that they are making progress.

Whenever you are checking the learning, make sure you let your child use some form of help, such as help sheets. **Looking at the help sheet is not "cheating". It is consolidating the learning wherever it is needed.** Examples of help to provide are detailed in the different activity descriptions.

Encourage and praise your child a lot. Suggest little challenges from time to time to check if you can go onto something more complex.

In his Ted Talk mentioned earlier[4], Mark Rober refers to an experiment he did with his YouTube followers. He presented it as a game to prove that anyone could learn to code. In the game, the participants had to enter commands to make a car go from the start line to the finish line. 1500 people took the challenge. Everyone started off with 200 points. After each failed attempt, half of them would read the message "That didn't work. Please try again". And for the other half, the message would say "That didn't work. You lost 5 points. You now have 195 points. Please try again".

The results showed that 68% of the participants who had no penalties managed to complete the challenge, and only 52% of those who lost 5 points after each failure did. The 16% difference was due to the number of attempts. On average, the "no penalty" group tried 12 times, compared to 5 for those who were penalised.

This experiment clearly shows that the way a failure is perceived can influence dramatically the way a learner reacts.

---

[4] Rober, M. (2018). The Super Mario Effect – Tricking Your Brain into Learning More. Accessed August 28th 2020 through https://www.youtube.com/watch?v=9vJRopau0g0

" This is perfect! You're so clever!"

As parents, we play a very important role in shaping the way our children handle failure. In her book, *Mindset*[5], Dr Carol Dweck demonstrates the subtle nuances in praise that can have a dramatic impact. With her research team, she has conducted the following experiment with four hundred 5th grade pupils across the United States. The children had to take several tests and were praised in two different ways.

The first test was very easy. Half of the students were praised for their intelligence: "You must be very smart". The other half was praised for their effort: "You must have worked very hard at this".

When given the option to take a second test that was either harder or easier, only 33% of the group praised for their intelligence chose the harder version and 92% of the group who was praised for their effort did. Dr Dweck explains this dramatic difference by saying that when praised for their intelligence or ability, a child (or adult) thinks: "Oh, you think I'm brilliant and talented. That's why you admire me – that's why you value me. I'd better not do anything that will disprove this evaluation". Consequently, they learn to play it safe, which in turn, limits their growth and their talent. However, by focusing on the strategies they use, the way they are stretching themselves, and taking on hard tasks, they think "If I don't take on hard things and stick to them, I'm not going to grow".

After taking a test that the children would surely fail at, the group praised for their effort worked harder, longer, and enjoyed it more. On the other hand, those praised for their intelligence became frustrated and tended to give up early.

The third test was the same as the first one. The overall result of the group praised for their intelligence went DOWN by about 20%, whereas the group praise for the effort went UP by nearly 30%.

This staggering 50% difference proves how much nurturing a "growth mindset" as Dr Dweck calls it, plays a part in a learner's learning journey. A growth mindset thrives on challenges, and sees failure as an opportunity to learn, stretch

---

[5] Dweck, C., *Mindset – Changing the way you think to fulfil your potential.* 2nd Edition, New York, Robinson, 2017, Chapter 7.

its abilities, and grow. For more information regarding this topic, you are kindly invited to read *Mindset* by Dr Carol Dweck.

To put it simply, praise the process and effort, not the intelligence or abilities. Please do keep in mind that the task presented to your child needs to be challenging but doable. The feedback you give will determine whether your child wants to carry on or quit. We must praise the effort and the process, and celebrate the failures. "Oh! This is good! What can we learn from that?"

"I told you TEN times already! How come you still can't remember?!"
Repeat, repeat, and repeat! No one can remember everything they were only told once. Let's remember that we are not computers. It is not because we have put a piece of information in our brain once that we can retrieve it anytime we want to or need to. In other words, it is not, for example, because you have told your child that a certain letter is pronounced in a certain way that they will remember the next time they see it. BE PATIENT!

It is a good idea to reinforce a piece of information in different ways i.e. different games, different sensory channels (visual, auditory, and kinaesthetic[6]), and in different contexts.

"Well, that's the way it is. You just need to remember."
When learning a new writing system, the shapes of the characters might be different, and/or the rules that govern their combinations might differ from the language they can already read and write in.

If you are introducing a new writing system, you will find various ways to familiarise your child with the new shapes in chapter 2: *How to start*. You can also refer to the various activities described in *The Toolbox for Multilingual Families* (2020) by Ana Elisa Miranda and Dr Ute Limacher-Riebold

Then it is a matter of familiarising your child with the way the home language is written through a variety of activities. **Repetition is key**! The unfamiliar will become familiar little by little.

---

[6] See glossary at the back for an explanation (p222-226).

"I know it's boring. But you need to make an effort."

Ignite interest and get your child involved emotionally! These are the best ways for learning to happen.

When it comes to random facts, people will generally remember those that pick their **curiosity** the most, they find the most **interesting**, or they can **relate** to the most.

Let's have a little experiment. Here are five random facts about languages. Read them, and see those that correspond to the explanation above, and in a few days or a few weeks, check those you can still remember. (If needed, on the last page of this book, you will find prompts and questions to help you remember them.)

1) The most translated book is the Bible. The second one is *Le Petit Prince* (*The Little Prince*) by Antoine de Saint-Exupéry (in 2017 it had been translated in 300 languages and dialects)[7].
2) Although the average adult knows passively (i.e. understands but does not necessarily use) 40,000 words, 1,000 of them represent 89% of the words used in everyday writing.[8]
3) Spanish contains about 4,000 Arabic words[9].
4) The Hawaiian language counts over 200 words to refer to the rain[10].
5) Cambodian has the longest alphabet with 74 characters[11].

---

[7] 'Le Petit Prince' (2020) Wikipedia. Available at: https://fr.wikipedia.org/wiki/Le_Petit_Prince (Accessed: December 26 2020)

[8] De Leon Huld, N. (2017). How Many Words Does the Average Person Know. Accessed December 26 2020 through https://wordcounter.io/blog/how-many-words-does-the-average-person-know/

[9] 'Arabic language influence on the Spanish language' (2020) Wikipedia. Available at: https://en.wikipedia.org/wiki/Arabic_language_influence_on_the_Spanish_language (Accessed: August 30 2020)

[10] Dekneef, M. (2016). Hawaiians have more than 200 words for rain. Accessed August 30 2020 through https://www.hawaiimagazine.com/content/hawaiians-have-more-200-words-rain

[11] 'Alphabet' (2020) Wikipedia. Available at: https://en.wikipedia.org/wiki/Alphabet (Accessed: December 26 2020)

"You understand this. So how come you can't do that?!"

As adults, we often forget how difficult it has been to learn new skills that now seem so natural, such as reading and writing. Transferring knowledge to different contexts is also very complex. Managing to apply what we have learnt to various contexts is the proof that the concept has been learnt and understood well. In order to enable your child to transfer what they have learnt to different contexts, it will take time, practice, and patience.

If your child cannot complete an activity, you will need to figure out what can be done to best prepare them for the activity. Here are some questions you could ask yourself:

- Is your child simply not understanding what is asked of them?
- Have they forgotten or misunderstood the instructions?
- Did you give too many instructions at a time?
- Are they misunderstanding a few words?
- Is the activity too mature?
- Do they remember the alphabet/ letter/word meaning?

This is why in this book, each activity provides ideas of support or ways to simplify the activity, as well as more challenging variations.

If the language you are teaching your child is a foreign language to you, do not compare the speed at which you have learnt that language to your child's progress. Please remember as well that adults are better equipped and progress more quickly[12].

III) When should I start to teach my child to read and write?

Different countries start teaching children to read and write at different ages. In countries such as the United Kingdom, the United States, and Australia, it can be as young as 4. In Finland, they start at 7 years old. Please, do not start off this

[12] Syafiyah, S. (2011). Are Children Better at Learning Languages than Adults? LiNGUA Jurnal Ilmu Bahasa dan Sastra 1(1) : 89-97

journey to biliteracy (or multilingual literacy) with thoughts beginning with "They need to ..." or "They should ...". Only start when your child shows interest. This is the key ingredient that will lead to success. Read a lot to and with your child, in their different languages, and create an atmosphere where reading becomes synonymous of pleasure. You will then see when your child wants to start understanding what is written in the home language. For ideas on how to start teaching your child to read and write, explore the next chapter, *How to Start*, and refer to the videos on www.library4multilinguals.com.

IV) It's all about LEVERAGE

If your child has already learnt or is currently learning to read and write in the school language, the first thing you can **leverage** is all the **groundwork** done by the schoolteacher to explain that the **"scribbles" on paper are representations of sounds and spoken words**. You will not need to explain again this visual-auditory link (whether your home language uses similar letters and characters or not) and you will be able to build upon that.

Leverage their knowledge of the language: You do not always need to teach everything, such as how to read a letter/character before they encounter it. Because they know the words in the home language, if they can read most words in a sentence, they can **work out** from the context how to read the new combination of letters, or the new character. You can then reinforce this discovery (that your child will be proud of!) and explain it. This process is also how we guess the meaning of difficult words in a text.

Leverage your child's interest. What are they interested in, passionate about, obsessed with? By being emotionally driven your child will put more effort in the task and the whole teaching/learning process will go much more smoothly. It is also important to make what they are learning **relevant** to them! The more it is linked to their universe (family, friends, interests) the clearer it is for your child to see the usefulness of learning it. As the parent, you can devise personalised activities, which is something that a teacher in a class setting can only do up to a certain extent. As their parent, you know better than anyone what your child loves. Use it to increase the engagement. If they like certain animals, include them in the games you will discover in the rest of this book. If they are obsessed with a particular cartoon, use its characters!

Leverage the emotional engagement! Learning does not need to be done sitting at a desk, and it certainly does not need to be boring! The activities included in this book are all language based but will primarily appear as games and fun activities in order to emotionally engage your child. They will consequently be more focused and should retain more.

To find more detailed explanations and precise examples of how to use these different ways to leverage the learning, head to www.library4multilinguals.com and check out the video titled *Leveraged learning*.

V) Mindset for parents

You do not have to stick to your plan to reach your goal:

If you are reading this book, one of your goals is to make sure your child can read and write in their home languages. Maybe your plan to achieve this goal is to work on these languages three times a week, or maybe you have enrolled your child on a certain course. If it appears like the schedule you have put in place is not manageable timewise, or the course is at a level that is not adequate for your child, do not despair! It does not mean that the goal will not be achieved. It just means that this way to achieve it might not be the right one. Do some research, reach out to other parents, and be inspired by them (online communities are great for that), there are certainly more ways to reach a goal than there can first appear to be.

Let your child guide you:

Provide ways to learn that will suit your child.

- **Interest**: If your child is interested in animals, a certain cartoon, astronomy, or anything else, find resources that are based on these topics.
- **Type of resources**: Your child will have preferences in the type of activities they like to do. Incorporate the literacy in there! If your child loves cooking, why not write the recipe of a dish, or cake you loved as a child and follow the instructions together?
- **The right moment:** Learning to read and write is a mentally very demanding task. Make sure you adapt the type of activity to the mental energy required. And remember that if your child is not in the mood, chances are that they will be reluctant to do the activity you are providing. As a result, the learning will not be as enjoyable and fruitful as it could be.

"Rome was not built in one day":

Remember that learning to read and write in the home language is a long-term game. There will be moments of slow progress, and others when you and your child will see rapid growth. Depending on the language and the exposure to it, it might only take a few weeks or months for your child to start deciphering words. **But it will take years for your child to become a confident reader and writer**. The most difficult part will be to sustain the effort long enough. (This is why this book has been compiled with fun and engaging activities. It will help make the journey more pleasant and will therefore help your child to carry on practising.)

Always make sure to remember how much your child could read and write a few weeks, months, or years ago, for you and your child to realise the progress made.

Do not compare!

Do not compare your child to others, whether they are monolingual or bi/multilingual.

A monolingual child will, generally speaking, have much more exposure and opportunities to practise their language. So do not expect your child to be as skilled as if they were brought up in a country where their language was spoken and written everywhere.

Also keep in mind that every child is unique. Each child will have their own circumstances, personality, abilities, interests. DO NOT COMPARE YOUR CHILD WITH OTHERS! It is of course easier to say than to do. Focus on what your child can do, their progress, and above all, what makes them happy.

Do not ban the community language:

If your child can already read and write in the community language and is likely to be educated in that language for many years to come, it is advisable to let your child explore that language too. Instead of banning the language, encourage your child to also explore the home languages by presenting fun and interesting ways to do so. Dive into this book, and pick and choose the activities that will resonate the most with your child.

Banning something can only result in negative feelings. Encouraging by feeding your child's interests will empower them and will help them endorse confidently their bi/multilingual and bi/multicultural identity.

It is also important to mention that the literacy skills a child learns in the community/school language can easily be transferred to the home language too.

CHAPTER 2 - How to start

I) Introducing a new script.

When teaching your child to read and write in the home language, you want the right "hook" to draw their attention and make them want to carry on! Learning to read and write will be a long process, so we need to make the journey as interesting and fun as possible. Like when you meet someone for the first time, the first impression is crucial.

The aim of this chapter is to give you a few ideas regarding how you can introduce a new script to your child in a way that will create a positive feeling about the journey ahead.

The first step is often the most daunting one. How can you start when your child does not know any letters? If you have been reading books in the language you are now going to teach, keep in mind that they will be familiar with the general shapes of the written form of the language. If your child has never seen this language written, it is a good idea to start by getting your child familiar with it.

Before anything else, read books together and comment on the way the language looks and comment on the script. Follow with your finger where you are reading. This will draw the focus to the way the language is written. In languages where the direction of the writing is different such as Arabic or Japanese, the attention will immediately be drawn to this "unusual" characteristic. This could be a starting point leading to questions from your child. Let your child ask you or tell you things that come to mind. This curiosity will become a driving force to the learning process.

You could encourage further exploration of the letters by asking questions such as:

- "Look at this letter! What does it look like?"
  → It might be a letter that looks like a letter they know in the community/school language.
  → It can have a funny shape that looks like an animal or an object.

By telling your child what these letters sound like, they are already learning how to read! These will be letters that they will recognise very easily.

- "Which letter do you like? / do you think has a funny shape?" Use vocabulary that will keep the exploration of this new script fun and positive.

How to start teaching the new script

Determine a first group of letters that you will teach in one go. The amount can vary from a few, up to nine. More than nine would make it challenging.

Keep in mind that you do not have to follow the order of the alphabet. It can be very efficient to determine this first group of letters/characters by their relevance and the way you want to introduce them.

Generally, when introducing a new script, we tend to go from the single letter/character to then combining them, up to the word level. In this section, you will discover two less-traditional ways to introduce letters/characters. (It is important to note that this approach is more effective if your child is already familiar with another writing system.) Both ways start at a word level to go little by little to the single letter/character level. They are using your child's ability to work things out to learn new things. For example, in Korean, a child might know that a "bee" is [bɒl][13] (벌) and "fire" is [bul] (불). By analysing (together) the differences, they can work out that the character ㅓ represent the sound [ɒ] and

---

[13] See the International Phonetic Alphabet if necessary (p227-228)

ㅜ is [u]. And if you also introduce the word 말 it becomes more obvious that the common sound [l] is written ㄹ.

This way of familiarising a child with a new script also has the potential to develop your child's confidence as it will leverage their previous knowledge i.e. the words in the home language and what they have learnt about reading in the school language. What they will learn will therefore seem familiar.

A) Contextualising the letters – the example of Korean

Short explanation about the writing system:

Like in the Latin alphabet Korean is written with a combination of vowels and consonants.

The modern Hangul alphabet contains 24 basic letters: 14 consonant letters (ㄱ ㄴ ㄷ ㄹ ㅁ ㅂ ㅅ ㅇ ㅈ ㅊ ㅋ ㅌ ㅍ ㅎ) and 10 vowel letters (ㅏ ㅑ ㅓ ㅕ ㅗ ㅛ ㅜ ㅠ ㅡ ㅣ).

There are also 27 complex letters formed by combining the basic letters: 5 doubled consonant letters (ㄲ ㄸ ㅃ ㅆ ㅉ), 11 complex consonant letters (ㄳ ㄵ ㄶ ㄺ ㄻ ㄼ ㄽ ㄾ ㄿ ㅀ ㅄ) and 11 complex vowel letters (ㅐ ㅒ ㅔ ㅖ ㅘ ㅙ ㅚ ㅝ ㅞ ㅟ ㅢ).

Although the position of the letter in the syllable can modify slightly its pronunciation, let's simplify it by saying that each letter has only one way to be read. (Contrary to Korean, in English for example, a letter can be pronounced in various ways. E.g.: "s" can be pronounced [s] as in "six" or [ʃ] as in "sugar".)

How to start:

You can choose to teach the vowels first (ㅏ ㅓ ㅗ ㅜ ㅐ ㅔ ㅡ ㅣ) as they are present in every word. They are therefore easy to encounter and essential to master. (Please have a look at www.library4multilinguals.com to watch videos explaining how I have introduced Korean to my son).

Problems: Many look very similar. You want to attach meaning to these letters so that they are both more memorable and can have an image attached to it (more meaningful and compelling).

Solution: Include these letters in SHORT words your child knows (e.g.: animals). This allows you to add shapes to these vowels that look so similar. Each vowel will then be associated with a word. Therefore, on top of the shape and sound of the vowel, you are now associating a meaning and an image, making the whole much more memorable.

<u>First activity to discover the vowels:</u>

Have a set of cards with a picture and the word written on them.	Have the words only written on a separate sheet.
	벌 말 금 게 잎 배 꽃 불

Ask your child to match the cards with the words on the other sheet and ask "So, how do you read this word?".

The aim is to get your child familiar with the general shape of the word and to associate the vowel with it. Note that the vowels are highlighted in red in order to draw attention to them. With multiple repetition games described in chapter 3 as well as in the detailed videos at www.library4multilinguals.com (see *Introduction to reading and writing in* Korean) you can make these words, reference words. While consolidating their knowledge of the letters, these associations help your child remember how to read them.

B) Starting off with a game – the example of Japanese

Explanation of the Japanese writing system:

Unlike the Latin alphabet, Japanese is not made out of combinations of consonants and vowels. It combines three writing systems: *hiragana*[14] (46 characters), *katakana* (used only for foreign words and names - 47 characters), and *kanji*[15] (these are Chinese characters. One needs to be able to recognise about 2000 to be able to read the newspaper and most books)

Hiragana and *katakana*: They are called "syllabic kana" and not alphabets, as each character is a syllable.

Kanji: Each character expresses an idea (logographic writing system).

How to start teaching hiragana

You can choose to select characters that make different words.

For example: うえ(up) した(down) みぎ(right) ひだり(left)

These words can be the basis for a nice little game and counts nine different *hiragana*.

Step 1: *Stand opposite your child and play a "Simon says" type of game with the directions.* (Watch the video *Introducing the Japanese Writing System* at www.library4multilinguals.com)

Remind/teach your child how to say these directions in Japanese (or your home language). You then point in a direction and say the word. Your child copies you. Please be aware that for "right" and "left" you will need to point in the opposite direction for your child to be able to copy you as a reflection in a mirror.

You can then play a *Simon Says* type of activity: When you do not say the correct word with the direction you are showing (e.g.: you point "up" but say した (down)) your child needs to be quiet, or they lose.

Step 2: *Introduce the script.*

Doing that on a support such as Powerpoint will be much easier (You can find a powerpoint in Japanese accompanying the video mentioned above, and

---

[14] See glossary at the back for an explanation (p222-226).

[15] See glossary at the back for an explanation (p222-226).

replace the words with any language you wish). You play the same *Simon Says* type game but instead of you pointing at the different directions, the words are written in Japanese (or your home language).

FIRST: The **arrows** and the **location** help to start associating the written words with the meanings and sounds. Your child relies mainly on the arrow. The attention to the written word is minimal.	うえ ひだり みぎ した
THEN: The **location** still helps your child. The attention to the written word is increased. At least the fact that one word (left) has three characters is more obvious.	うえ ひだり みぎ した
FINALLY; On the Powerpoint, the words appear and disappear in different places of the screen. The attention to **details of the words** is increased.	うえ ひだり うえ うえ ひだり みぎ うえ みぎ ひだり ひだり うえ みぎ みぎ した ひだり した みぎ ひだり した した みぎ した した

<u>Step 3</u>: *Help your child work out the way to read each letter/character on its own by finding them in the* hiragana *grid.*

The *hiragana* grid is traditionally presented as below and can easily be considered a table with two entries. You can therefore guide your child in finding the common sound per column and per line. Note that this is an activity where your child will be able to leverage their knowledge of the writing system of the community/school language (if based on consonants and vowels)

Start with the *hiragana* discovered in the games in the previous steps, and others your child might know already. Once you have at least three in the same column or row, the pattern starts to be visible, and you can annotate with your child the entries of each column and row for your child to then work out how to pronounce all the other letters in the grid.

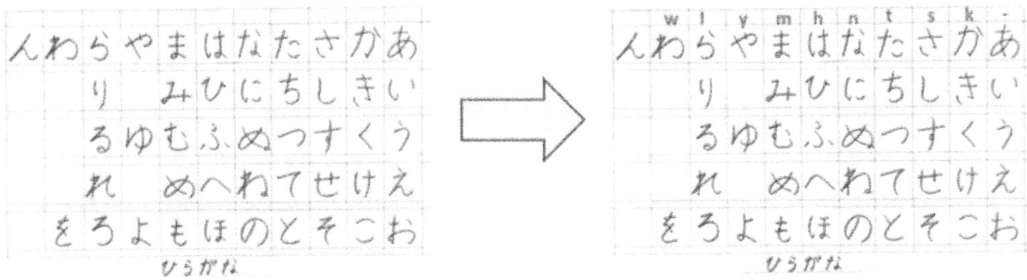

II) How to start teaching a language with the same writing system.

When you teach your child to read in a language that uses a similar writing system to the one they have already learnt, the building blocks are already in place. It is therefore "just" a matter of teaching how some letters sound differently and how there are different letter combinations.

As explained on pp 28-29 you can start by introducing letters with words rather than as isolated letters to provide each letter with something that carries meaning rather than just a sound. If the letter can be read in multiple ways, use words that contain the most straightforward reading. For example, in English, the letter "a" can be read [a][16] as in "cat", [ɑ] as in "arm", [eɪ] as in "baby", and if combined with other letters, it can be read in many other ways!

The first thing to do is to help your child understand that they can already decipher most of the words, and that there are only a few tricky bits to learn.

Should you use capital letters or lowercase letters?

There are two schools of thought regarding this question. By looking at the examples below, you can notice that a word written with capital letters appears as a rectangle, whereas the same word written in lowercase has a more distinctive shape.

---

[16] Please refer to the International Phonetic Alphabet (IPA) chart at the back p227-228.

CAR EYE BUT car eye but

ALPHABET alphabet

There are advantages to both ways of presenting the words.

- With a word written in capital letters, your child will have to focus on each letter at a time to decipher it.
- With lowercase letters, the overall shape of a word is more distinctive and will therefore help your child remember its spelling. This will later help them read faster. However, it must be stressed that whole word recognition can easily lead a child to guess the words based on their overall shape. It is therefore recommended to balance activities at a letter, syllable, word, and sentence level. (This book displays a variety of activities focusing on each level).

Here are a few ideas to start:

A) Card game to discover the language:

Choose about nine to twelve words. Three or four must be very transparent (i.e. not containing combinations of letters that are different from the language your child can already read), and the rest can contain combinations of letters you want to introduce and work on. You do not need to include a different combination of letters per card. Three different combinations repeated on different cards is a good number to start with.

The cards below can for example be used with a child who can read English confidently and is learning to read in French.

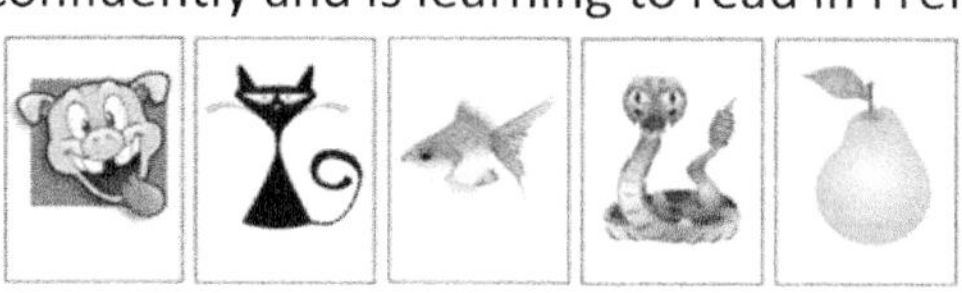

un cochon	un chat	un poisson	un serpent	une poire

un bonbon	un robot	un canard	un piano	une peluche

The transparent words are "robot", "canard", and "piano".

The other cards contain the following combinations that you can start showing directly: ch / on / en / un / oi. Although there are five combinations, "ch" and "on" sound very similar to the way they are pronounced in English, and therefore do not make it too difficult to remember straight away. The trickier combinations are "en", "un", and "oi".

Step 1: *Only show the pictures and ask your child what each picture represents.*

This is for you to check that each picture is clear, and that your child knows them in the home language. It also ensures that when your child will read the words, they know they are written in the home language.

Step 2: *Keep the cards with images randomly spread out in front of your child and give your child the cards that have words with transparent spelling. Ask them to match them with the corresponding image.*

This should be easy and boost your child's confidence. The only tricky part will be the article that might be pronounced [yn] instead of [œ̃][17]. Just ask casually in the home language "Do we say 'une robot' or 'un robot'?" to help them remember what sounds correct. If your child chooses the wrong gender, you can simply explain that "un" is pronounced [œ̃] but "une" is pronounced [yn] and show another card.

As most cards start with the article "un", this combination will be remembered in no time.

Step 3: *Put the other word cards in front of your child to match them with the images*. Keep "un poisson", "un serpent", and "une poire" with you as they have the most complex combinations.

Depending on how confident your child is, you could help them:

- either by pointing at a picture that corresponds to an easier word (e.g.: "un bonbon, une peluche, un cochon") and trying to find the word card based on the first sounds of the words.

[17] Please refer to the International Phonetic Alphabet (IPA) chart at the back (p227-228)

- or by taking an easy word card and sounding out the beginning to guide your child to find the right picture.

The aim here, is to help your child **work out** the new combinations of letters specific to French (or your home language).

Congratulate your child on the feat! This is a great achievement! Remember to underline the process of working out rather than praising their intelligence or ability (see p19)

Step 4: Once all the cards are matched, summarise the new combinations of sounds discovered, and reinforce the learning.

You can for example:

- ask your child to group together all the cards that have a certain sound.
- write on a mini whiteboard, a word and substitute syllables by others to form different words.

E.g.: ***p***oire → ***b***oire → **b**oisson → **p**oisson ; cochon → ***co***ton → ***cha***ton → bâton ; ***ch***at → ***r***at

B) Leverage technology

One of the first signs I saw, telling me that my son wanted to learn to read and write in French, was that he wanted to send messages to my French family. (In the past, he had wanted to do it in English, the language he learnt to read and write in school, but that was the first time he asked to do it in French).

The Predictive Text on phones can do wonders to help children to get a first taste of how to read and write in a language that has a similar alphabet to the one they know already.

The advantage of the predictive text is that while typing, it gives you several options to choose from. This means that:

- your child does not need to know exactly how to write a word and can write by recognising the one they need, which is a much more achievable task.
- tricky combinations of letters and silent letters can be seen, discussed, and reinforced by repetition.

- your child can start getting familiar with the fact that some letters are not pronounced similarly between languages E.g.: the letter "j" is pronounced [dʒ][18] in English (e.g.: **j**uice, **J**apan) but [X] in Spanish (e.g.: mo**j**ito, **j**alapeño pepper).
- It can often give points of discussions. E.g.: In French, "c'est" (meaning "it is") pronounced [se], has quite a tricky spelling. My son used to write it "se" which is a word that exists in French but that is pronounced [sə]. The high frequency of "c'est" enabled my son to remember the spelling very quickly.

Tip: You do not want your child to be discouraged by the fact that there are many words that do not look like they sound. Try to simplify or choose alternatives to reduce the difficulty of working out the words due to their "tricky" spelling.

C) Short children's book

Depending on your child's age, you might be able to introduce reading and writing through children's books that contain little writing. They are aimed at monolingual children. The content will therefore match the age group at which children start to read in the country of the language. If the age difference is too big, these books might not interest your child too much. However, if your child is close to that age group, these books will constitute great resources.

Here are their advantages:

- They are short so offer a rapid sense of accomplishment.
- They generally have a very repetitive structure. Therefore, the number of words to discover is little. You will need to work together to decipher the words the first time, but your child will feel rapidly more confident. The more they encounter them and the easier it will be to read them.
- You can comment on the pictures and talk about the story.

Keep in mind that this activity is not supposed to be fully focused on reading. It is meant to familiarise your child softly to a new writing system.

---

[18] Please refer to the International Phonetic Alphabet (IPA) chart p227-228.

To start with, you can start by reading and only leaving the transparent words for your child to read. Even the transparent words will include specific sounds of the language. Here is an example in English, French, Spanish, Italian, and German: chameleon, caméléon, camaleón, camaleonte, Chamäleon. They are all very similar but will be pronounced slightly differently. Compare the pronunciation of the word between the home language and the way it is written and pronounced in the language your child can already read in.

III) Now that I have started, what next?

Once you have started in a positive way, it is important to keep it going. At the beginning, it is crucial that you let your child guide you. In other words, adapt the practice to your child's taste and interest. This will ensure your child wants to keep having fun with you in the home language and will help the momentum going. If you feel like a certain structure, a routine, is to be put in place, make sure to do it in discussion with your child so that it does not feel imposed. The activities in the rest of the book will help you provide a variety of activities to get the practice going, in an enjoyable way for your child.

This book is here to provide options. It should not be used as the only source to teach your child to read and write.

Your child's interest in being able to read and write in your home language will be nurtured by seeing the purpose and the enjoyment these skills procure. An easy way to do this is to read together regularly. You can for example have a "bedtime story" routine. This will create some quality time reinforcing the parent-child bond that will consequently help your child feel your language as important in their eyes.

Encourage your child to read in **any** language. This will nurture a love for reading that will be extrapolated to other languages. A child who does not like to read will face both the complexity of the task and will be forcing themself to read. Reading will then turn into a chore! A child who loves to read will be driven by their positive emotions, wanting to know more about the content of the book. The difficulty to read in the home language will only constitute a mere obstacle to overcome in order to get to the anticipated joy!

CHAPTER 3 – Games and Activities to practise reading and writing single letters or words.

Explanations about the games and activities

In this chapter, you will discover 70+ games and activities for your child to practise reading and writing in a fun and engaging way. As a parent, your aim is to make your child literate in the home language(s). These games are designed to practise reading and writing in ways that will engage them, and perfect their skills as a consequence.

The activities are divided into three sub-sections: single letters or words; short sentences; short texts. Each sub-section contains reading activities first, and then writing activities.

Note that even when your child can already read texts, you can still play with single words to reinforce their knowledge of the spelling or meaning of words. Variations of the activities are also explained so that you can reuse a game that your child loves by adapting it to their level.

Each activity displays the following:

- **Name of the activity**
- **Preparation time:** 🕐 (up to 10 min); 🕐🕐 (up to 30 min); 🕐🕐🕐 (more than 30 min) – On the website (www.library4multilinguals.com), you can

find a RESOURCES PACK that accompanies this book with templates to reduce the preparation time, and videos explaining how to adapt the resources.

- **Minimum level of mastery of the language required**: ☆ beginner / small amount of vocabulary known required; ☆☆ (Close to) age-appropriate amount of vocabulary known; ☆☆☆ Good range of vocabulary known.
  🕮 Just starting to be able to decipher letters and words; 🕮🕮 Starting to confidently decipher words; 🕮🕮🕮 Emergent reader and confident reader / writer.
  Please keep in mind that most games are presented with variations to adapt to your child's level.
- **Minimum number of participants**
- **Material required**: Most activities can be played with objects you would already have at home. The RESOURCES PACK also provides templates.
- **Aim of the activity**
- **Instructions for the activity**
- **Learning process and why it works**
- **Illustration**: Most games and activities have illustrations to clarify them.
- **Variation(s) of the game**: This section details ways to increase or reduce the challenge of the game to adapt to your child's needs (see point made below about challenges). It can also contain variations that present the activity in a different way but that will have a similar learning outcome for your child.

What is the right amount of challenge?

For your child to learn and enjoy the activities, it is important that the right amount of challenge is provided. Too easy, and no learning will take place (although, it can also sometimes be an efficient way to show your child how much they have progressed!). Too hard, and your child will be discouraged and might even give up. Please note that you do not need to always introduce new words, rules, etc. **Revisiting what has been previously learnt is very important as it consolidates the learning**. Retrieving from memory is an important part of the learning process.

As mentioned in chapter 1 in the section *Common teaching mistakes*, help sheets and other support are necessary to bring your child up to mastering new knowledge. You want to encourage your child to remember and not always glance at the help provided. However, until they are confident, do let your child access it. Each time they use the help sheet, it consolidates the learning. This will also help you assess more accurately your child's level of mastery.

Creating multi-purpose material.

Creating material can be very time consuming. You want to make the material appealing enough so that your child likes it, but you do not want to spend hours creating something that will only be used once. This is why it is very important to create material that can have multiple uses. (If you know it is likely to be an activity your child will only play once, you DO NOT need to make it look pretty!!) Cards are a prime example.

Tip to make them versatile: Always keep the image and the word on separate cards.

<u>List of possible Games</u>	Image and word together on the card	Image and word on separate cards	
(see details of the games in the rest of the book)	 un poisson		un poisson
The odd one out	✓	✓	
Hit the card	✓	✓	
Memory	✓	✓	
Pick and Match		✓	
Mastermind		✓	
Spot the missing one		✓	
Match the cards		✓	
Domino		✓	

I) Single letters or words

When a child starts to learn to read and write in a language, it can be quite daunting. And when they can already do that in the school/community language, going back to square one with another language can be quite off-putting. Why would they bother going through the struggle again?! This is why it is very important to introduce it in a fun and engaging way. Luckily, you have 30+ activities to choose from.

Many simple games (that you probably know) are already fun to play. By tweaking them a little, you can easily help your child to practise their reading and writing skills.

Reading

#1 Noughts and Crosses / Tic-Tac-Toe

Preparation time:	**Minimum level of mastery of the language required**
Minimum number of participants: 2	**Material required**: Pen Paper
Aim of the activity: Deciphering words and reinforcing the knowledge of the spelling by reading them over and over.	

<u>**Instructions for the activity:**</u>

- Draw a small grid with nine boxes.
- In each box, write the letter or the word you are practising. This might also be a particular character/phonic/letter you are teaching your child to read. (See the examples below)
- In turns, each player needs to read the word before drawing a circle or a cross in the box read.

<u>***Example with letters:***</u>	<u>***Example with words:***</u>
Reading Japanese *hiragana* In this grid the *hiragana* make the words うえ(up) した(down) みぎ (right) ひだり (left) (Refer to Chapter 2: I) *Introducing a new script / B) Starting off with a game*)	Working on how to read the letter "s" in French, that can be pronounced [s] or [z]. As much as possible, keep the words easy to read. Only introduce one difficulty at a time.

<u>**Learning process and why it works**</u>:

- This is a <u>recognition activity</u> where your child, who has already learnt what is present in the grid, will be reinforcing their knowledge.
- This activity is perfect for beginner readers as the amount to read is minimal. Your choice of words or characters can focus on one area (e.g.: one phoneme[19] or grapheme[20], words related to one topic, etc.)
- The competitive nature of this game will encourage your child to pay attention to the details (e.g.: shape of the letters, rules explaining how to read a word, etc.)

<u>**Variations**</u>:

Support:

- You can keep help sheets nearby to support your child. Referring to help sheets will reinforce their learning.

Challenge!

- You can have, as a rule, to only be able to draw the circle or the cross if the letter/word is read correctly. Please, keep in mind that you DO NOT want to pressure your child negatively. Help your child to read the words if needed, but this added rule can motivate your child to make more effort to read the word/character correctly.

---

[19] See glossary at the back for an explanation (p222-226).

[20] See glossary at the back for an explanation (p222-226).

#2 Memory

Preparation time:	**Minimum level of mastery of the language required**
	/
Minimum number of participants: 2	**Material required**: One set of word cards One set of picture cards You can create your own set of cards (please see the RESOURCES PACK on www.library4multilinguals.com).
Aim of the activity: Deciphering words and reinforcing the knowledge of the spelling by reading them over and over.	

Preparation of the material:

- Have a set of cards with pictures only, and another set with words only (as explained in Chapter 3 / Creating multi-purpose material)
- The number of cards used in the game needs to be adapted to the level of mastery of the language and the age of the youngest player.

Instructions for the activity:

- Place all the cards face down. Have the picture cards on one side, and the word cards on the other side.
- Each player, in turns, picks one picture card and one word card, and sees if the word written on one card matches the picture on the other one.
- If they match, the player keeps the cards. If they do not match, the cards need to be placed face back down (in the same place).

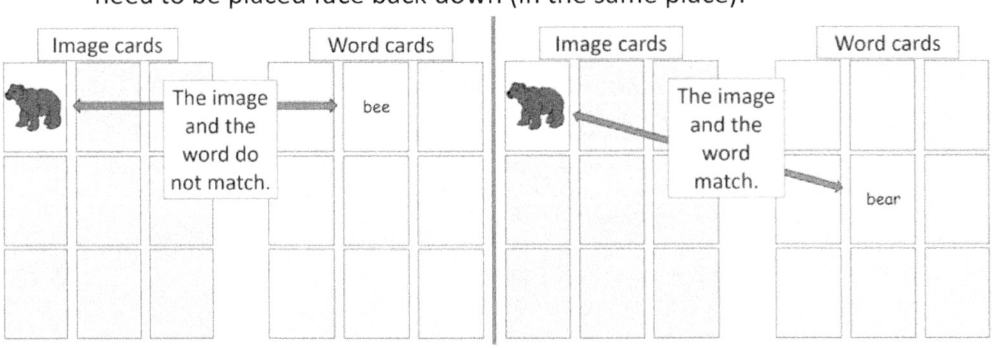

Learning process and why it works:

- In order to match the pairs, the player will have to read over and over the same words. This repetition coupled with the competitive nature of the game will help your child practise reading in an enjoyable and effective way.
- Please, keep in mind that this game needs to support your child's learning. Therefore, the game should not contain too many words/characters your child does not know or cannot read.
- Including a couple of new letter combinations (or characters) could be a great opportunity to teach new ones. Teach your child the first time the word card is turned over, during the game. Motivated by the game, your child will get familiar very quickly.

Variations:

Support:

- If your child is still deciphering words, you can have a sheet with pictures and the words written underneath. Your child will be able to refer to it and by reading it over and over, it will reinforce the learning.

Challenge!

- To increase the difficulty of the game for more confident readers, use this game to revisit a wider range of phonics/words/characters. You can also include new phonics/words/characters that will be taught while playing.

#3 Bingo

<table>
<tr><td>Preparation time:</td><td>Minimum level of mastery of the language required
☆/</td></tr>
<tr><td>Minimum number of participants: 3</td><td>Material required: Pen
Paper</td></tr>
<tr><td colspan="2">Aim of the activity: Deciphering words and reinforcing the knowledge of the spelling by reading them over and over.</td></tr>
</table>

Preparation of the resources:

- Prepare a list of vocabulary/characters/letters that you have either been working on with your child, or that your child can decipher. If the list is extensive, make sure you order or group the words logically so that they can be found quickly. You can for example order them alphabetically, or group them by words containing similar sounds.

Instructions for the activity:

- Ask your child/all the players to pick a set number of the words from the list by circling them. E.g.: your child chooses くま (bear)、あひる (duck)、いぬ(dog)、うま (horse)、ひつじ (sheep)、りす (squirrel) (see next page)
- You start reading out loud the words from the list in a random order e.g.: うし (cow), さる (monkey), あひる (duck), ぶた (pig), りす (squirrel), きつね (fox) ...
- When your child has heard all the words they had chosen, they shout "BINGO!" (in the example on the next page, あひる(duck) and りす (squirrel) are ticked off as they are the words you have mentioned.

Note that it is even more enjoyable if there are several players and one gets all the words first!

<table>
<tr><td>List you provide your child to circle the words.</td><td>Help sheet – See "Variations" section.</td></tr>
<tr><td>Your child chooses a few words from the list by circling them. They can tick off the words you say.

</td><td>
</td></tr>
</table>

<u>Learning process and why it works:</u>

- The list of words can be as short as a dozen, or relatively extensive, and can therefore adapt to various demands in terms of reading practice.
- This activity primarily focuses on the link between the way a word sounds, and its visual representation (phoneme-grapheme[21] correspondence for languages with an alphabet). Your child will need to read the words in order to spot the one being said by you.
- As your child only needs to check if you are saying the words they have circled, they can only focus on the few words they have chosen, the

[21] See glossary at the back for an explanation (p222-226).

amount to read is quite restricted, making it perfect for children starting to decipher letters and words.

- The competitive nature of the game will help your child pay attention to the details of the way a word is spelled/written.
  Note that due to the random nature of this game (the words are picked randomly) it is ideal if you are working with children that are at different levels of mastery of the language or reading ability. Indeed, the reading speed or proficiency does not determine the winner.

Variations:

- If you are on your own, with one child, you can write all the words on separate cards (or use a set of picture cards), put them in a pile, face down. You or your child then turn the card on the top of the pile, and your child (or you) reads the word out loud. Each player ticks off the words if they are on their lists.
- You can also make this game more kinaesthetic[22] by choosing objects or toys you put in a bag. Your child puts their hand in the bag to pick one object randomly.
  → Please note that this can also give them a chance to "cheat" as they can feel the object before taking it out. From a learning point of view, this is not a problem at all because in order to choose an object, your child would have read the word first. The aim of this activity is to encourage your child to read!

Support:

- If your child is still deciphering words, you can have a sheet with pictures with the words written next to them. Your child will first recognise the word being said, will look for the picture on the sheet, then see how it is written, and finally will try to find the similar word on their Bingo grid.

[22] See glossary at the back for an explanation (p222-226).

- By providing a list of words with pictures, you can also ask your child/the players to copy the words they want on a separate sheet. This step will add writing practice.

Challenge!

- Include words spelled/written similarly so that your child needs to pay attention to the details. It is also a good idea to include homophones[23] so that your child sees that different spellings refer to different meanings. When mentioning them, make sure to include them in sentences for your child to understand which homophone you meant.

[23] See glossary at the back for an explanation (p222-226).

#4 Connect 4

Preparation time:	**Minimum level of mastery of the language required**
Minimum number of participants: 2	**Material required**: Connect 4 game Paper + Blue tack Alternatively: Post-it notes
Aim of the activity: Deciphering words and reinforcing the knowledge of the spelling by reading them over and over.	

Preparation of the material:

- Cut seven square pieces of paper that are the width of a column of the game.
- On both sides of each piece of paper, write a word. It should be the same word on each side. In total you need seven different words.
- Stick them at the top of each column. Make sure that the words are easily legible by both players. (see illustration below)

Instructions for the activity:

- The aim of the game is to get four pieces of your colour in a row (horizontally, vertically, or diagonally)

- In order to place a piece in a certain column, the player needs to read the word stuck at the top of the column correctly.
- If the player does not read the word correctly, they cannot place the piece in that column, and the other player can play. The aim of this added rule compared to the original game is to incentivise your child in paying attention to read the words/characters properly. Reinforce this rule at the beginning of the game when there is nothing at stake, but make sure you support your child throughout the game when playing.

Learning process and why it works:

- The small number of words/letters/characters your child needs to focus on, and the repetitive nature of the game will help them consolidate their learning.

Variations:

Support:

- If you are working on letters, and have previously introduced a letter associated with a certain word, have a sheet with the pictures and the associated letters together. If you are working on a particular phoneme[24] or way to sound a letter out, let your child have access to the material they previously used to learn them.

  The retrieval process[25] your child will be going through will reinforce the learning each time.

Challenge!

- When you feel like a word is becoming too easy to read for your child, either swap the words around (if you are only focusing on seven items), or replace them by others.

---

[24] See glossary at the back for an explanation (p222-226).
[25] See glossary at the back for an explanation (p222-226).

#5 Bowling

Preparation time:	Minimum level of mastery of the language required
🕒🕒	☆/ 📖
Minimum number of participants: 1	**Material required**: 10 empty paper cups. Pen Paper Tennis ball
Aim of the activity: Deciphering words/single letters/characters	

Preparation of the resources:

- Prepare between 10 and 30 papers. Write one word/letter/character on each of them.
- Place them inside the paper cups. There should be one paper per cup.
- Place the cups in a triangle shape, like bowling pins.

Instructions for the activity:

- One player throws two balls at them and tries to knock down as many cups as possible.
- The player needs to read the words placed in each cup that fell over. Each cup that fell is one point, and each word read properly adds an extra point.
- The aim is to get as many points as possible.

Your child reads the words inside the fallen cups.

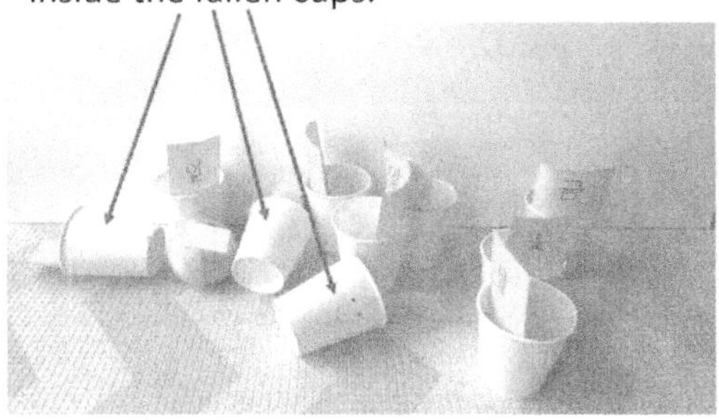

Note: You can decide beforehand on different prizes. The higher the score, the better the prize! If there are more than one player, you can either add the points of each player so that they work collaboratively, or you can organise it as a competition. (For a positive experience for all players, the collaborative model is advised)

Learning process and why it works:

- Your child is incentivised to read the words by the fact that they can win more points.
- Remember to help your child decode the words/letters/characters, by referring to help sheets. The aim is to help your child read in an encouraging environment, and not to catch them whenever a word is not read properly.
- It is a good idea to involve your child in writing the words on the papers. This creates a sense of ownership over the activity. It also gives your child a chance to go over the words before playing the game, and therefore revise the different combinations of letters they are going to need to read.

Variations:

Support:

- Have a help sheet accessible. This could be a sheet you previously used to explain how to read a letter in certain contexts, or have the words written under the pictures representing them. Let your child have access to the material they previously used to learn them. **The retrieval process**[26] your child will be going through will reinforce the learning each time.

Challenge!

- You can write sentences.
- It is a great opportunity to incorporate some numeracy. On each paper, below the word, write a number or an operation. This number or result can be added to the score if the word is read properly, or subtracted if it is not read correctly.

---

[26] See glossary at the back for an explanation (p222-226).

#6 Secret Wax Message

Preparation time: 🕐	Minimum level of mastery of the language required ☆/🕮
Minimum number of participants: 1	**Material required**: white sheets of paper paint white candle stick or white crayon
Aim of the activity: Deciphering words/single letters/characters	

Preparation of the resources:

- ① On a few sheets of paper, write words/letters/characters with the white candle stick. (You should barely be able to see the words)

Instructions for the activity:

- ② Present the activity as a normal painting activity to your child, and ask him to paint a beautiful rainbow for example (or anything else that requires lines going across the paper).
- ③ + ④ The paint will not stick to the paper where the wax is. Your child will discover in amazement the word you previously wrote appears!
- ⑤ Now explain to your child how to do it and let them write words they like, for you to discover while painting.

1 Write the secret message.

2 Let your child paint as they wish.

3 They will start distinguishing words.

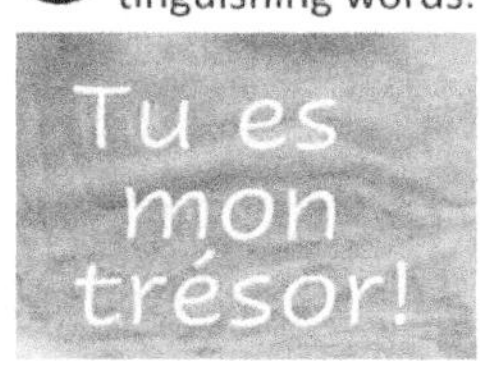

4 Message discovered and decorated.

5 Let your child write a secret message.

Learning process and why it works:

- Having a hidden message revealed makes the discovery of the word interesting, and might lead your child to want to write some themself.
- The word appears little by little and therefore points at different details of the words. The attention to details plays an important role to master reading and writing.

Variations:

- You can write a word in the corner of the sheet (e.g.: lion) and then draw a lion's head on the rest of the sheet. Ask your child to first read the word. Then they can paint the rest of the page to see if they read the word properly.
  Alternatively, if you do not draw very well, ask your child to first paint the page to guess your drawing. Then they can reveal the answer by painting the word.

Challenge!

- Include words your child has not seen written before but is able to decipher.

#7 Back Writing

Preparation time: ◷	Minimum level of mastery of the language required ☆/ 📖
Minimum number of participants: 2	**Material required**: None
Aim of the activity: Focusing on the details of each word/character. This exercise reinforces their visual representation.	

Preparation of the resources:

- This is a "zero preparation needed" game.

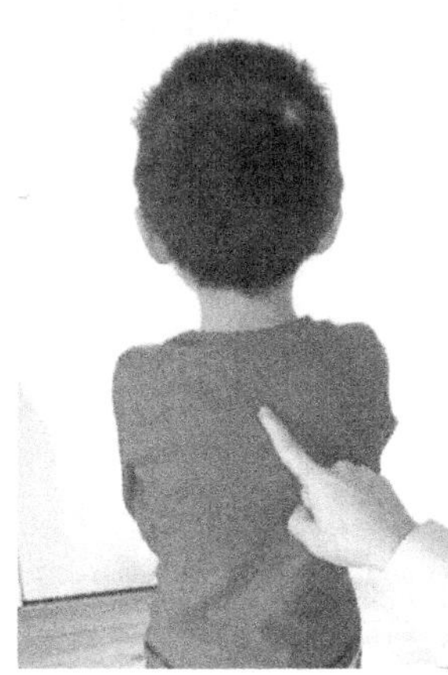

Instructions for the activity:

- With your finger, write a word/character on your child's back.
- They need to work out the word/character you wrote and say it out loud.

Learning process and why it works:

- Your child pictures in their mind the word/character you wrote. The attention put on each detail helps your child remember the spelling (or the shapes of the letters and characters) better.

Variations:

- You can organise it as a Chinese whisper game with 4+ people in a line. The first one decides on a word (and writes it on a piece of paper) and then writes it on the back of the second person. The chain carries on up to the last person in the line, who needs to say the word out loud.

Support:

- For children who are not yet confident readers and writers, use shorter words (or simpler characters)

Challenge!

- Write longer words.
- If your child can read and write in two or more languages that use the same script, do not mention the language the word is in.

#8 Spot the Missing One

Preparation time:	**Minimum level of mastery of the language required**
Minimum number of participants: 2	**Material required**: Word cards Picture cards Tray (If you already have a set of word cards and picture cards, the preparation time goes down to zero).
Aim of the activity: Deciphering words.	

Preparation of the resources:

- An ideal number of words/characters to work with is between 5 and 9. The more confident and the older your child is, the more words you can have.
- Have word cards displayed randomly on a table.
- Before starting the game, ask your child to match the word cards with the picture cards to make sure that they know which word goes with which image. It is also an opportunity to help your child be aware of the words they are playing with.

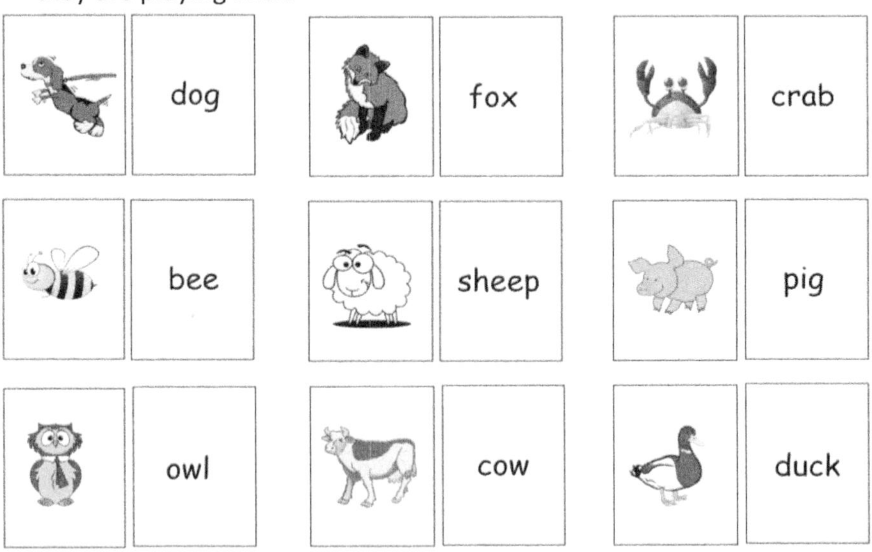

Instructions for the activity:

- The picture cards are placed in front of your child. Further, place the word cards randomly.
- Place the tray between the words and the pictures and remove one word card. (While removing a word card, feel free to mix up the other ones)
- Remove the tray and your child needs to spot the missing word.

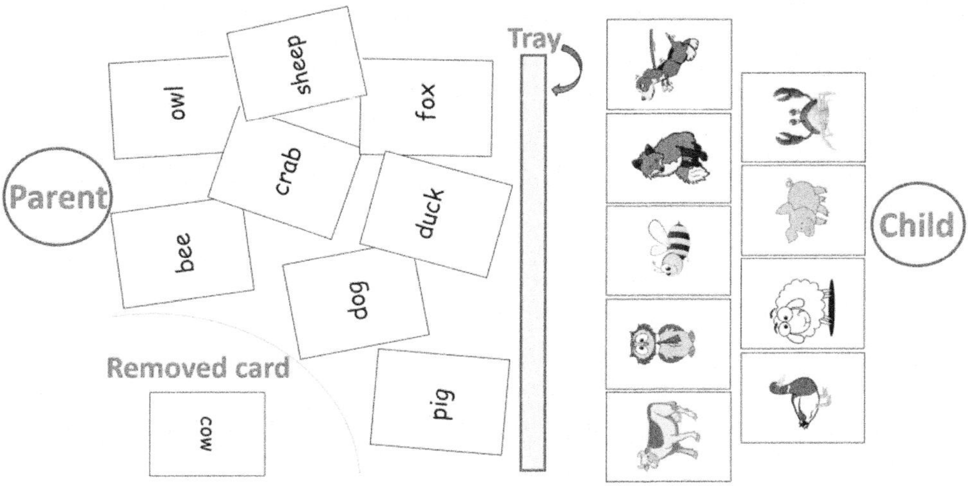

Learning process and why it works:

- Your child needs to read the words over and over to make sure they spot the missing one.
- Matching the words present with the images is one exercise, but realising that one of the pictures does not have a matching word will help their brain retrieve the spelling of the word from their memory.

Variations:

Support:

- Instead of picture cards, give your child a sheet with the words and images together.

Challenge!

- Set a timer to limit the time available to find the missing word.

#9 Wordsearch

Preparation time: ⏲	**Minimum level of mastery of the language required** ☆/ 📖
Minimum number of participants: 1	**Material required:** Printer Internet connection
Aim of the activity: Spelling. Paying attention to the order of the letters.	

Preparation of the resources:

- Create a wordsearch by using one of the numerous websites that already exist. You can easily find one by searching for "wordsearch generator" online.
- Alternatively, you can create your own one. Simply draw a grid with 15 to 20 square boxes. Write words horizontally and vertically, with one letter in each box. Then fill the rest of the grid with random letters. It would take you the same amount of time.
- Above or next to the grid, write a list of words you want your child to find.

Fill the grid with the words you want your child to find.

Bear
Chameleon
Duck
Eagle
Elephant
Flamingo
Forest
Tiger
Rhinoceros
Snake

										e	a	g	l	e
	d	u	c	k										
				b	e	a	r							
					l									
	f				e									
	l				p			f	o	r	e	s	t	
	a				h		c						i	
	m				a		h						g	
	i				n		a						e	
	n				t		m					s	r	
	g						e					n		
	o						l					a		
	r	h	i	n	o	c	e	r	o	s		k		
							o					e		
							n							

Add random letters all around.
Your child will need to find the words amongst all the letters.

Bear
Chameleon
Duck
Eagle
Elephant
Flamingo
Forest
Tiger
Rhinoceros
Snake

l	o	y	e	s	t	t	a	r	b	e	a	g	l	e
l	d	u	c	k	t	a	j	b	n	d	t	u	e	o
e	e	a	s	b	e	a	r	j	o	y	r	e	s	t
y	b	a	e	r	l	r	p	s	t	s	e	j	i	n
o	f	u	l	r	e	s	t	b	o	u	d	u	e	o
u	l	b	v	d	p	o	k	f	o	r	e	s	t	c
j	a	l	r	e	h	t	c	e	a	r	d	b	i	l
i	m	a	b	r	a	s	h	d	f	l	r	e	g	t
n	i	r	e	s	n	n	a	o	s	f	l	r	e	s
d	n	h	i	n	t	c	m	f	l	r	e	s	r	y
s	g	y	r	h	i	n	e	c	e	r	o	n	d	b
b	o	k	r	h	c	i	l	o	c	e	r	a	s	t
g	r	h	i	n	o	c	e	r	o	s	d	k	l	r
r	u	c	p	h	i	n	o	c	e	r	o	e	r	w
l	o	r	d	r	h	i	n	o	c	e	r	o	s	i

Instructions for the activity:

- Your child needs to find all the words in the grid.

Learning process and why it works:

- This is a fantastic activity to reinforce spelling and attention to details.
- Your child needs to find amongst all these letters the right combination of letters. They need to pay attention to the right succession of letters.

Variations:

Simpler version:

- Write the same word over and over again, and have some of the words spelled incorrectly (e.g.: the letters are not in the right order, letters are missing)

Example with the word "magnificent"

m	a	g	n	i	f	i	c	e	n
t	m	a	n	g	i	f	i	c	e
n	t	m	a	g	n	i	f	c	e
m	a	g	i	f	i	c	e	n	t
m	a	g	n	i	f	i	c	e	n
t	m	a	g	n	i	f	i	c	a
n	t	m	a	n	g	i	f	i	c
e	n	t	m	g	n	i	f	i	c
m	a	g	n	i	f	i	c	e	n
t	m	a	g	n	i	j	i	c	e

Challenge!

- For learners who can already spell quite confidently and have a wide range of vocabulary: Either put pictures of the words you want your child to find, or simply do not write any list so your child needs to look at the letters and find out those that could be combined into words.

<u>**Particular examples**</u>:

- Some languages such as Japanese can be written in different ways. In that case, choose the most appropriate writing system.

E.g.: The Japanese *hiragana*[27] and *katakana* characters each represent a syllable. However, with *kanji*[28] (Chinese characters used in Japanese) each character represents an idea and can be a word (or part of a word) on its own. Therefore, *hiragana* and *katakana* are more suited to the wordsearch activity. (If working with *kanji*, the grid could contain similar looking characters.)

<table>
<tr><td>STEP 1: Find the words in the grid (written using hiragana).</td><td>STEP2: Write the words in the second writing system (in kanji in this example)</td></tr>
<tr><td>Below, the list of words to find are represented by pictures.
For clarity, the darker characters (hiragana) represent the answers. (Two words are already circled as examples)
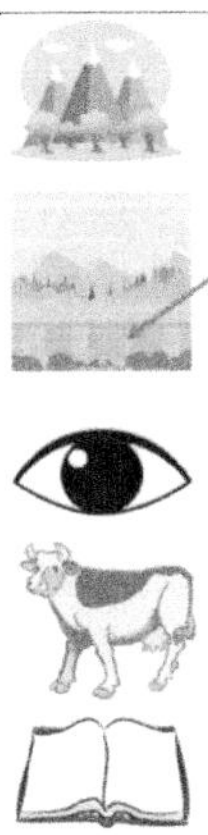
<table><tr><td>よ</td><td>め</td><td>れ</td><td>う</td><td>し</td></tr><tr><td>ぬ</td><td>ね</td><td>じ</td><td>ら</td><td>ぼ</td></tr><tr><td>か</td><td>わ</td><td>が</td><td>ほ</td><td>や</td></tr><tr><td>よ</td><td>す</td><td>ほ</td><td>れ</td><td>ま</td></tr><tr><td>ぬ</td><td>は</td><td>ん</td><td>じ</td><td>ぼ</td></tr></table></td><td>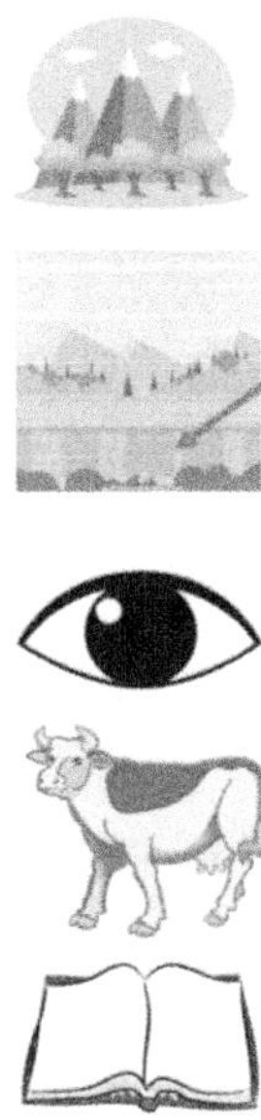
山
川
目
牛
本
<table><tr><td>よ</td><td>め</td><td>れ</td></tr><tr><td>ぬ</td><td>ね</td><td>じ</td></tr><tr><td>か</td><td>わ</td><td>が</td></tr><tr><td>よ</td><td>す</td><td>ほ</td></tr><tr><td>ぬ</td><td>は</td><td>ん</td></tr></table></td></tr>
</table>

[27] See glossary at the back for an explanation (p222-226).
[28] See glossary at the back for an explanation (p222-226).

- In certain languages the shape of characters/letters changes when you link them together to write a word. In Korean, the letters are placed next to or below each other when combined into characters.

E.g.: 벌 (a bee) is made up of three characters ㅂ, ㅓ and ㄹ that are combined both horizontally and vertically.

By placing them separately in the wordsearch grid, you help your child find all the necessary "components" in the place, before combining them. If your aim is to help your child learn to combine the characters, it is a good idea to provide the list of words to find as pictures.

<table>
<tr><th>STEP 1: Find the characters that make up each word.</th><th>STEP 2: Combine the letters.</th></tr>
<tr><td>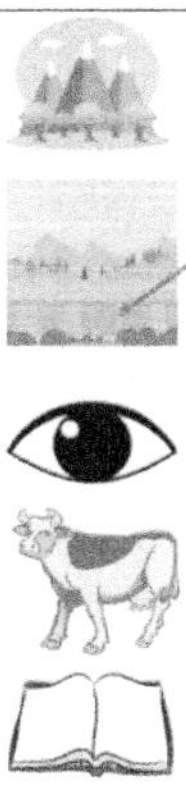 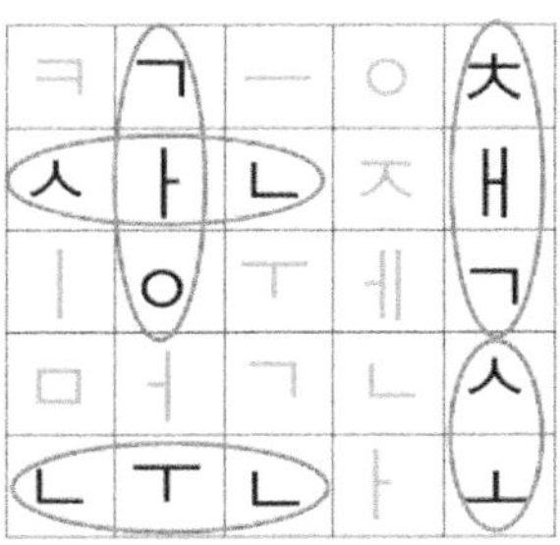
</td><td> 산  소
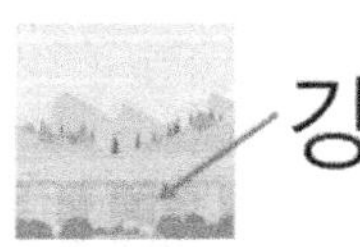 강  책
 눈</td></tr>
</table>

#10 Mastermind

Preparation time:	Minimum level of mastery of the language required
Minimum number of participants: 2	**Material required**: Picture cards Word cards (If you are reusing cards prepared for other games, the preparation time would be 0min)
Aim of the activity: Deciphering words and remembering them by repetition.	

Preparation of the resources:

- Choose about ten words you want to work with. You can either focus on a specific grapheme[29], letter, topic, or use this activity as a revision opportunity and therefore pick the words randomly.
- Have a set of cards with the words on them, and another set with the images representing these words.

Instructions for the activity:

- Give the picture cards to your child and keep the word cards.
- Your child needs to pick four cards that they place in a line and face down. The aim is for you to find the correct combination of cards i.e. the words corresponding to each picture, and in the right order.
- You place four word cards in a certain order, face up, for your child to read. They then tell you which word(s) is/are:
  - in the right position (represented by ✓ in the illustration below)
  - in the sequence they chose, but not in the right position (✓)
  - not part of their sequence (✗).
- You have up to fifteen tries to find the right combination.
- You can then swap roles.

[29] See glossary at the back for an explanation (p222-226).

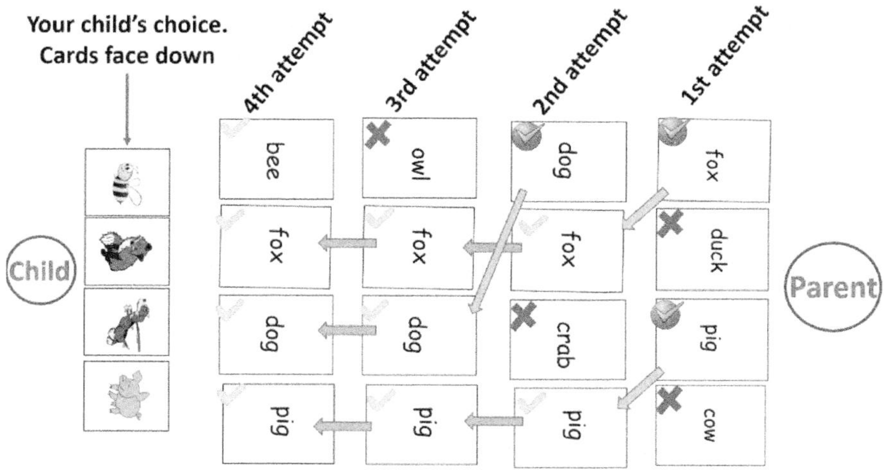

Tip: It can be difficult for younger children to keep track of the cards. It can therefore be a good idea to write on a piece of paper (or mini whiteboard) the different attempts using symbols (as pictured above).

Note that all the words are facing your child to help them read.

Learning process and why it works:

- Every time you place your cards down, your child will need to read them to see if they correspond to their combination. And when they will be the one choosing the cards to work out your combination, they will need to read the cards too. By seeing the same words over and over, your child will learn them seamlessly.

Variations:

- You can remove the limited number of tries to avoid any stress or frustration.
- You can limit the number of cards for the combination to three, and reduce the number of tries to ten.

Simpler version: The goal is to find the cards in the combination (in any order).

#11 The Treasure Hunt (Powerpoint)

Preparation time: ⌚⌚	**Minimum level of mastery of the language required** ☆/ 📖
Minimum number of participants: 1	**Material required**: Powerpoint / Google slides Template available in the RESOURCES PACK on www.library4multilinguals.com Alternatively: word cards and picture cards – see section "Variations" below.
Aim of the activity: Deciphering words.	

Preparation of the resources:

- Create a treasure hunt on a powerpoint (See the explanation video on www.library4multilinguals.com). It should include items your child knows already and is able to decipher.

Instructions for the activity:

- Establish different prizes for points your child earns in this game.
- Your child reads a word in the grid, then clicks on it to reveal the corresponding image.
- If the word is read correctly your child earns one point. If it is read incorrectly, it takes away one point.
- The final score reveals the prize your child won.

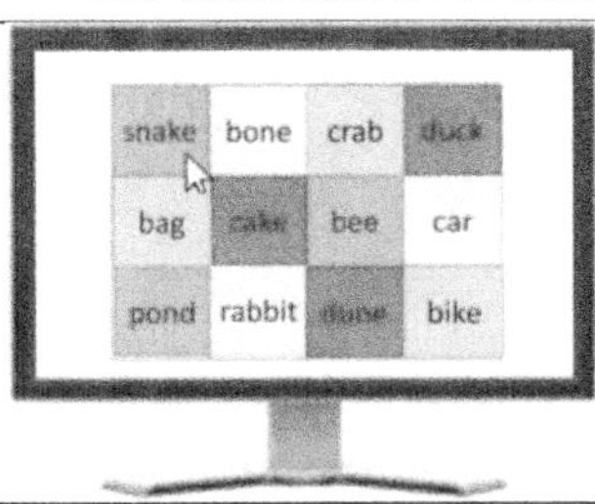

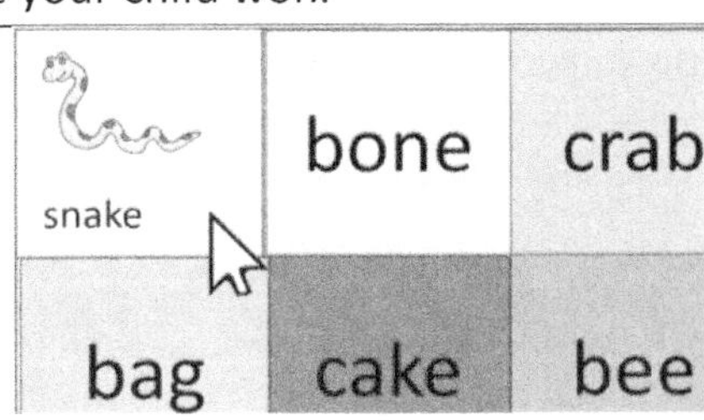

STEP 1: Your child reads a word. **STEP 2:** They click on the box.	**STEP 3:** The picture behind is revealed. If the word read matches the picture, your child earns a point. If the word does not match, they lose a point.

Learning process and why it works:

- Your child is free to choose whichever word they feel comfortable reading first, so they can go from the most familiar to the most unfamiliar ones. This keeps your child in control and helps build confidence.
- Once the easiest words are read, you can refer to them to help your child see that different words have similar letters/combinations of letters. This will help your child read more unfamiliar words too.
- The prize they can win is an incentive to help your child to keep going when it seems a little hard.

Variations:

- You can play this game using cards. Place the word card on top of the picture card so that it is not possible to see the picture at all. Once the word is read, remove the card to reveal the image below.

Support:

- Have the word written in the box next to or below the picture so that your child can refer to them and use them as references when deciphering unfamiliar words containing similar letters and combination of letters. (See example of "snake" on previous page)
- Alternatively, you can have a sheet with all the pictures that are in the game, and lines next to each picture. Each time a word is read, it needs to be written/copied on the line next to the correct picture.

The pictures will give your child a limited choice of possible answers and therefore will guide them when deciphering the words. E.g.: if the word is "elephant", and your child deciphered "ele-", by looking at the different pictures, they can realise that there is only one picture starting with "ele-

", and that is "elephant". You can then draw their attention to the fact that "ph" is read [f].

Challenge!

- Increase the number of unfamiliar words (that can be deciphered).
- Include numeracy by writing mathematical operations in each box. If the word was read properly, the result is added to the total score. And if the word is misread, it is deducted from the score. By including these operations, the game will become more unpredictable and will therefore make it a little more exciting.

 2x3 =	bone	crab	duck
bag	cake	 27-9 =	car
pond	 17+8 =	dune	bike

#12 Matching-up Treasure Hunt

Preparation time:	**Minimum level of mastery of the language required**
Minimum number of participants: 1	**Material required**: felt tip pen paper ruler printer (optional) blue tack or tape (optional) treasures (whatever your child will enjoy discovering)
Aim of the activity: Deciphering words/single letters/characters.	

Preparation of the resources:

- Hide a few treasures in your house.
- On an A4 sheet of paper, draw a floor plan of your house.
- On top of the floor plan, place another sheet of paper, and place them on a window (by day). The day light should help you see the floor plan through the plain paper. Mark with a pencil the locations of the treasures.
- Prepare twice as many word-image pairs as there are treasures hidden.
- Place the words and images on the plain sheet of paper so that by drawing straight lines to link the words with their corresponding images, two by two, the lines cross on the locations that mark the treasures.

(If necessary, refer to the video explanation available in the RESOURCES PACK. Please go to www.library4multilinguals.com to download it)

__Instructions for the activity:__

STEP 1: Ask your child to link the words with the corresponding pictures by drawing lines with a ruler and a dark coloured felt tip pen.

(In the example below, the images of "present" and "Christmas tree" are linked to the words in Korean.)

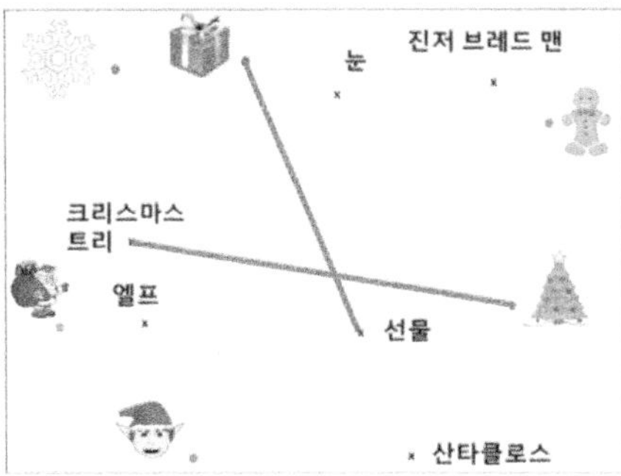

Here is an example of floor plan with some places and items in the house named (in Korean) to help your child orient themself.

STEP 2: Using blue tack or tape, your child sticks the sheet on a window and then places the floor plan over.

They should see the lines they drew on the match-up worksheet (in white on this example) through the floor plan.

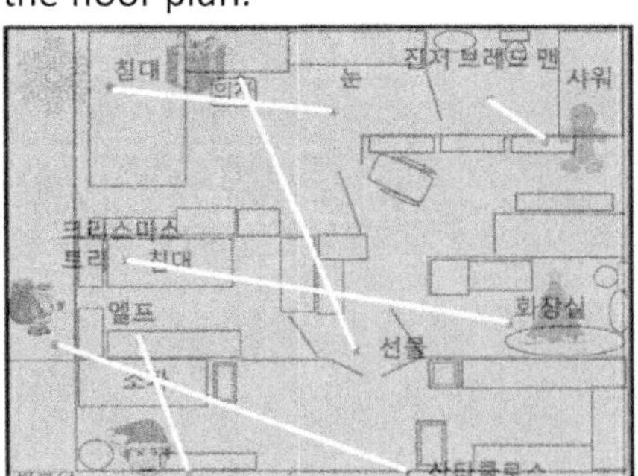

STEP 3: Your child marks the intersections (they see by transparency) on the floor plan.

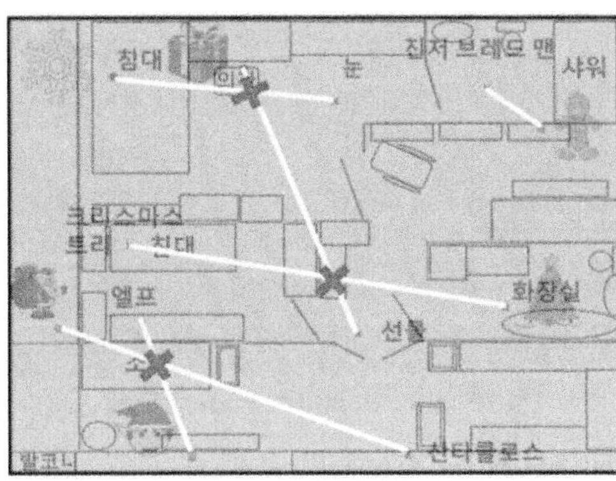

STEP 4: Let your child check if there are treasures hidden in the places indicated on the map. (Note that younger children will need help to orient themselves with the map.)

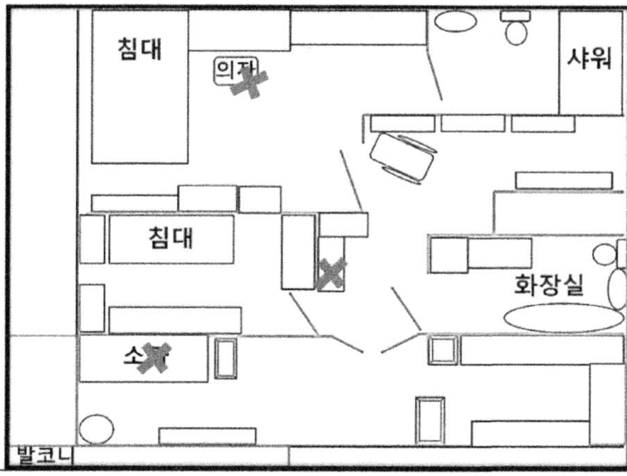

Learning process and why it works:

- This is a way to make the traditional matching-up exercise purposeful. Unless the words and pictures are matched correctly, the resulting intersections will indicate different places on the map and they will not find the treasures.

Variations:

Support:

- Have a help sheet accessible. This could be a sheet you previously used to explain how to read a letter in certain contexts. Let your child have access to the material they previously used to learn them. **The retrieval process**[30] your child will be going through will reinforce the learning each time.

Challenge!

- Include words your child has not seen written before but is able to decipher.
- Include more pictures than there are words (or vice versa) so that your child really needs to carefully read each word.

[30] See glossary at the back for an explanation (p222-226).

#13a The Jumping Frog

Preparation time: [clock icon]	**Minimum level of mastery of the language required** ☆/ [book icon]
Minimum number of participants: 2	**Material required**: Marker pen Masking tape Optional: cushions
Aim of the activity: Recognising globally how a word is written. (The more similar the spelling of the words, the more precise your child's knowledge needs to be)	

<u>**Preparation of the resources:**</u>

- Place different cushions on the floor. These represent water lilies.
- Write one word on a bit of masking tape, and place it on a cushion. Do the same for every cushion.

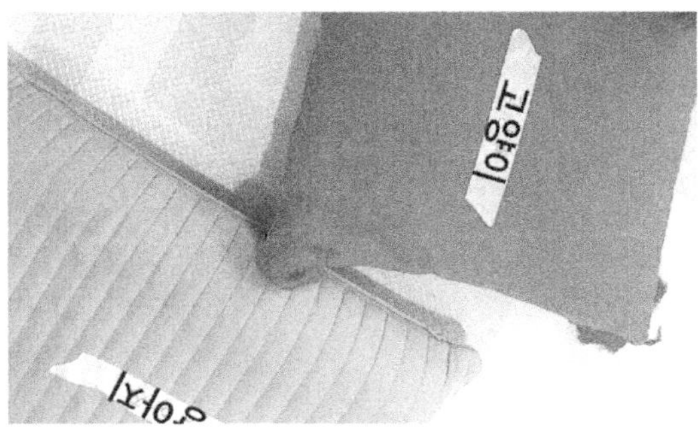

<u>**Instructions for the activity:**</u>

- You read out loud one of the words.
- Your child needs to jump on the corresponding cushion.

Learning process and why it works:

- This game allows repeated exposure to a word and will help memorising them.
- The more similar the spelling of the words, the more precise your child's knowledge needs to be (e.g.: letter, ladder, later / book, look, took, boat, link, etc.)

Variations:

- For older children, you can place the words on the circles of a Twister game. Say a sentence containing one or several of the words. Your child needs to jump on all the words one after the other.

Support:

- Have a help sheet with the images and the corresponding words written below.

Challenge!

- Your child needs to read the word before they jump on the cushion. However, they can only jump on the cushion/water lily if the word has been read correctly. You can also set a limited time for your child to be on a water lily. If the word is not read by the moment the time is up, the water lily "sinks in the water" and your child loses!
- Instead of masking tape, you write a word on the back of post-it notes that you stick on cushions. (The word is only visible once your child turns the post-it note over). Your child jumps on a cushion and has limited time to read the word.

#13b Hit the Card

Preparation time:	**Minimum level of mastery of the language required**
Minimum number of participants: 2	**Material required**: Word cards (or create your own) Note that although your child does not need to know many words, this game is based on speed. They should therefore be reasonably confident reading the words, if played as a competition between different people.
Aim of the activity: Recognising globally how a word is written. (The more similar the spelling of the words, the more precise your child's attention to details needs to be)	

<u>Preparation of the resources:</u>

- Create cards that are the size of playing cards.
- Write a word on each card.

<u>Instructions for the activity:</u>

- Place the word cards randomly on a table. Make sure that the words are facing your child to allow them to read them easily.
- You say a word, and your child needs to touch the correct word.
- In order to add an incentive, have a timer set to 3 minutes. Your child needs to hit as many correct cards as possible.

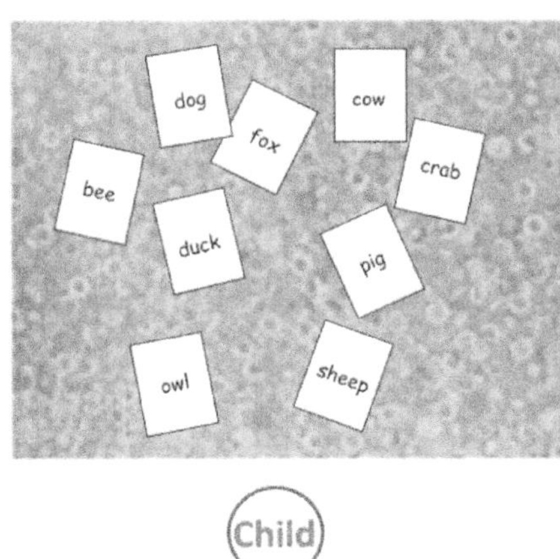

If you play this game with several players, make sure they have a similar reading level. Otherwise, the least comfortable reader will feel frustrated.

Learning process and why it works:

- This is a game that practises recognition of words and letters/characters. **This is a step up from deciphering words** and should only be played once your child can decipher words confidently enough.
- This will reinforce attention to details of the words and characters presented to recognise them quickly.
- This game will help children to decipher words quite confidently to recognise words as a whole. As mentioned earlier in the book, please make sure to write the words in lowercase so they have a more distinctive shape.

Variations:

- If you want to play it as a competition with your child, have a pile of picture cards (that correspond to the words on the table). The card should be placed face down. In turns, flip around the card on the top to discover the image of the word you need to hit first.

- If you are teaching letters, you can say words starting with one of the letters on the cards, and your child needs to hit the corresponding card. If you work at a word level, you can say a sentence containing one of the words on the cards. You can then reverse roles. Tip: Sometimes, make mistakes on purpose to see if your child can spot them.

Support:

- Give your child a sheet with the words and their corresponding images so that they can refer to it if necessary.

Challenge!

- Once your child becomes more confident reading the word, turn the cards so that they appear sideways or upside down. If you play with children who do not have the same reading level, the cards should be facing the child who is the least confident.

#14 Battleship

Preparation time:	**Minimum level of mastery of the language required**
Minimum number of participants: 2	**Material required**: 2 battleship grids 2 pencils
Aim of the activity: Reading a selected number of words and remembering them by repetition.	

Preparation of the resources:

- Create two identical tables with double entry.
- At the top of each column, write a word, and to the left of each line, write a word.

Instructions for the activity:

- Each player has a grid and places battleships on them. Some should cover 4 boxes, some 3, and some 2. The ships should cover about ¼ of the total number of boxes in the grid.
- The number of ships and their sizes needs to be agreed between the players.

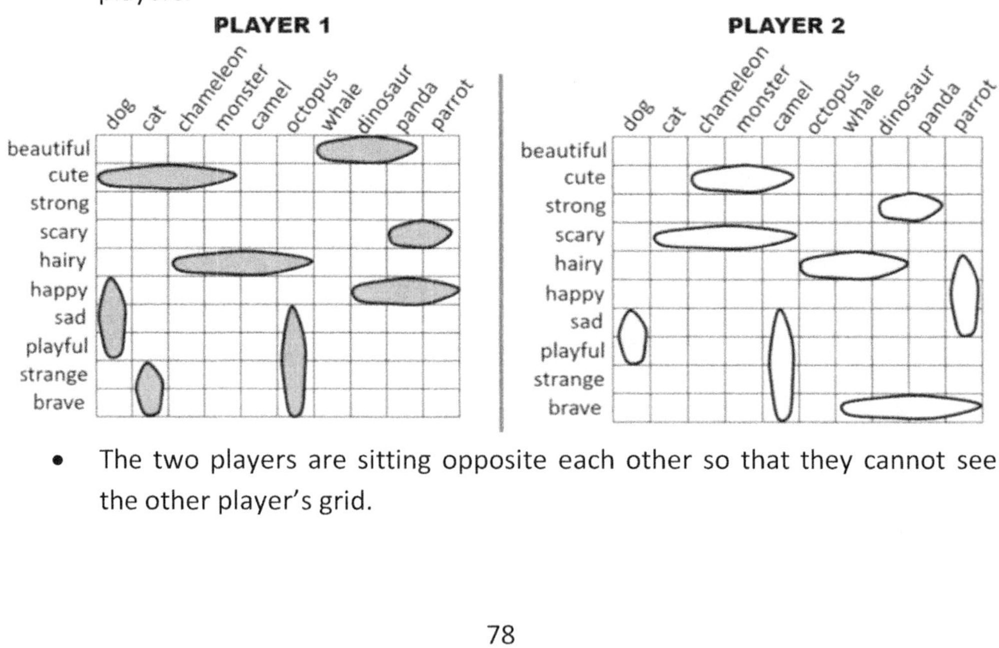

- The two players are sitting opposite each other so that they cannot see the other player's grid.

- In turns, the players read one word from the left and one from the top of the grid. They act as coordinates to point at one box.
- The aim is to sink your opponent's ships () before all yours are sunk.

Note 1: If you want to reinforce the order of words (e.g. noun and adjective), place the words to be said first on the left, and the words to be said second at the top (if the reading direction in your language is left to right), and encourage your child to say the words in the appropriate order. **E**.g.: "This is such a ______ ______". Your child will be encouraged to say sentences such as "This is such a *cute monster*".

Note 2: You can also play this game to reinforce the knowledge of some words and put images instead of words. Your child will then need to remember the words associated with each picture in the given language.

Note 3: You can practice conjugation and place the subject pronouns on the left and verbs in their infinitive form at the top. In order to point at a specific box, the verb needs to be conjugated correctly.

Learning process and why it works:

- To point at a certain box, your child will need to read the words appropriately. By reading them over and over, your child will remember them better. Misreading a word might lead to pointing at the wrong box, and therefore missing a shot.

Variations:

Support:

- You can have a separate sheet with the words written and the pictures representing them.

Challenge!

- You can write a sentence that contains two gaps. Each gap will correspond to a word (on the left and at the top of the grid).

#15 The Hungry Crocodile

Preparation time:	**Minimum level of mastery of the language required**
Minimum number of participants: 2	**Material required**: Mini whiteboard Whiteboard marker
Aim of the activity: Deciphering words / Focus on details to improve knowledge of spelling.	

Instructions for the activity:

- In one corner of the mini whiteboard, write a word. In the three other corners, write misspelled variations of the same word.
- Place your hand near the edge of the mini whiteboard, palm facing down, like a crocodile waiting for its prey.
- Say the word out loud.
- Your child needs to choose the right word.
  → If they pick the correctly spelled one, nothing happens.
  → If one of the misspelled ones is picked, you close the crocodile's mouth on their hand!
- If your child chose the wrong option, point at the letters that differ, and help your child work out why it is not the correct spelling (explain if necessary).

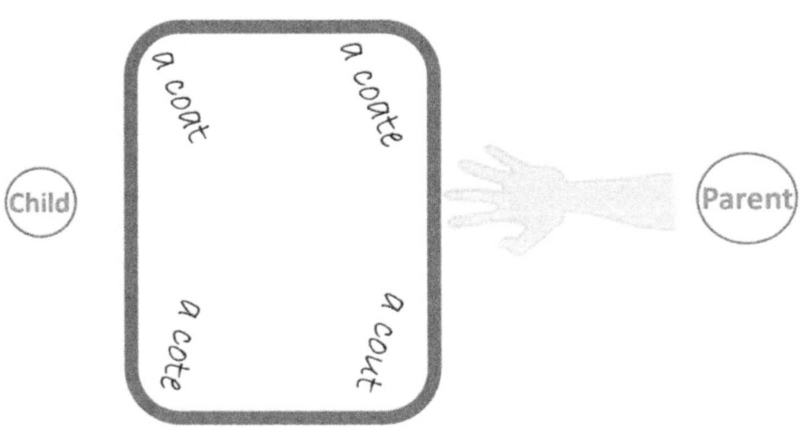

Learning process and why it works:

- The similarities between the different versions give options to choose from. This exercise is therefore easier than writing a word by trying to remember every detail (i.e. every letter and their order, or every stroke of a character).
- You can focus on specific orthographic[31] difficulties your child has, and have the correct spelling as well as misspelled variations.
- This is the opportunity to reinforce what has been previously learnt (e.g.: how to read particular letter combinations (graphemes[32]), where certain silent letters come from, the meaning of some parts of Chinese characters, etc.)

Variations:

- **Easier version**: Only write words that exist, and that are similar. There will be more visible differences.
- **Version with homophones[33]**: Write homophones. You say a sentence using one of them. Your child needs to touch the correct one.

Support:

- Leave next to the game any material, worksheet, lesson you have covered to refer to it if necessary, in order to reinforce the learning.

Challenge!

- Set a timer between 3 and 10 seconds. Your child needs to find the correct word before the time is up.

---

[31] See glossary at the back for an explanation (p222-226).
[32] See glossary at the back for an explanation (p222-226).
[33] See glossary at the back for an explanation (p222-226).

#16 Board game

Preparation time:	Minimum level of mastery of the language required
Minimum number of participants: 2	**Material required**: Dice Paper "Snakes and ladders" board game (Alternatively, find the board game pictured below in the RESOURCES PACK available on www.library4multilinguals.com
Aim of the activity: Deciphering words/single letters/characters	

Preparation of the resources:

- Create a list of words, and number them to associate each one with a numbered square on the board game (If your board game does not have numbered boxes, add the numbers by using post-it notes, for example).

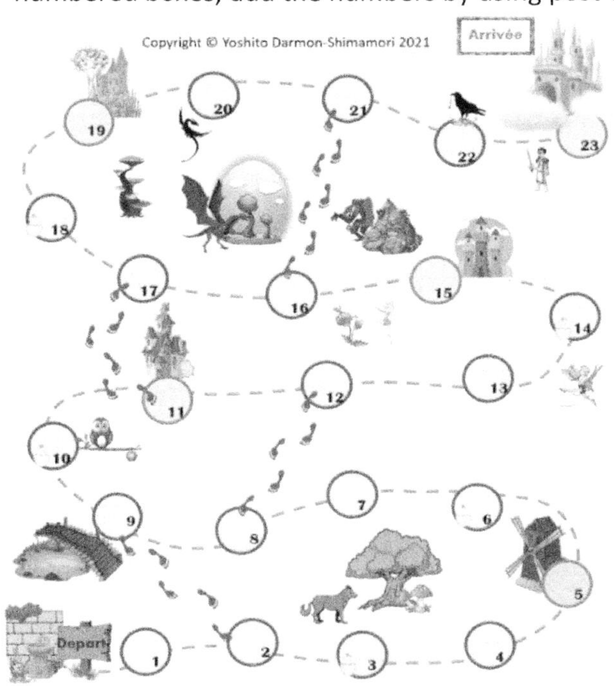

List

1. Un poisson

2. Un escargot

4. Un serpent

5. Une cerise

6. Un dessert

7. Une boisson

8. Un poison

10. Un aspirateur

11. Un désert

[...]

- The squares at the bottom of the ladder do not need any word, as the player goes up the ladder to read the word at the top. Similarly, the squares where the snakes' heads are do not need any word.

Note: On the board game pictured the footsteps going down act as snakes. The magic potions replace the ladders (For the complete rules, please check the RESOURCES PACK)

Instructions for the activity:

- Each player puts their counter on the space that says "start here" ("Départ" in the example is French).
- Take it in turns to roll the dice. Move your counter forward the number of spaces shown on the dice.
- If your counter lands at the bottom of a ladder, you can move up to the top (in the example above, a magic potion tele-transports you to the next square containing one). If your counter lands on the head of a snake, you must slide down to the bottom of it (or follow the footsteps in the example).
- Each time, read the word (on the list you created) corresponding to the number on the square you land. If the word is read correctly, you can stay. If not, you need to go back on the square you were on before rolling the dice. If you slide down a snake and cannot read the word, you must perform a dare given to you by the other players.
- The first player to get to the "home" square ("Arrivée" in the example) is the winner.

Learning process and why it works:

- This is a revision game and should only include items that your child is able to decipher/read.

- Seeing these words again in a playful environment will enable your child to remember the words better.
- Your child is motivated by the game to pay close attention to the details as they want to win.
- Your child's aim is to win the game, but your aim is to help your child improve their reading skills. Make sure you assist your child in reading the words.

<u>Variations</u>:

- If you want to work on writing as well as reading, every time a player lands on a snake or ladder, you can give them a few words to write that includes the specific item you are working on.

Support:

- Have a help sheet accessible. This could be a sheet you previously used to explain how to read a letter in certain contexts, or have the words written under the pictures representing them. Let your child have access to the material they previously used to learn them. **The retrieval process**[34] your child will be going through will reinforce the learning each time.

Challenge!

- Include words your child has not seen written before but is capable of deciphering.

<u>**Note**</u>: Remember that the aim of this game is to practise reading and writing in a fun way. If you see your child struggling, provide help by asking questions such as "The word '…' contains the same sound. Do you remember how to spell it?". This will avoid frustration and negative feelings towards reading and writing.

---

[34] See glossary at the back for an explanation (p222-226).

If you provide help and your child still gets it wrong, you put them in a situation where the goal was achievable. It is therefore much more likely that they take this failed attempt as a lesson for the next round, instead of feeling frustrated to have been given a task too difficult to be resolved.

With younger children, defeat is much harder to handle. Please use your own judgement as a parent.

#17 Pick and Match

Preparation time: (No preparation time needed if you already have the cards)	**Minimum level of mastery of the language required**
Minimum number of participants: 3	**Material required**: 1 set of word cards 1 set of picture cards 1 joker card Create your own cards (see explanation video on www.library4multilinguals.com) or use those provided in the RESOURCES PACK.
Aim of the activity: Deciphering words, and reinforcing their meaning.	

Preparation of the resources:

- Have a set of cards with pictures only, and another set with words only (as explained in Chapter 3 - *Creating multi-purpose material*).
- Have 4 pairs of cards per player, another 4 pairs for the stack, and one joker.
  → For 4 players, the game should therefore contain 20 pairs and 1 joker, i.e. 41 cards in total.

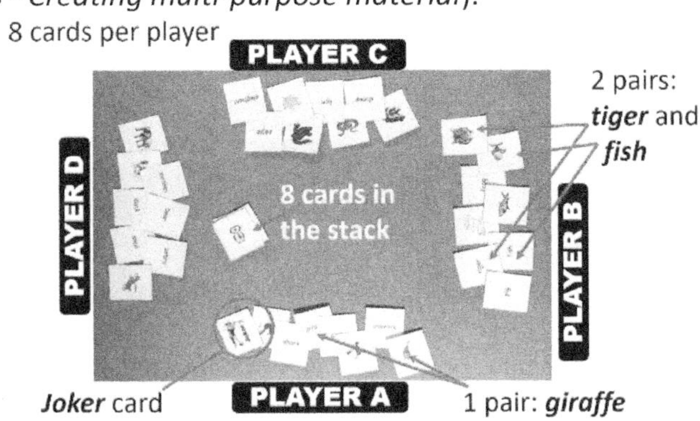

Instructions for the activity for 3+ players:

- Shuffle all the cards together (see picture above).
- Give out eight cards randomly to each player. The remaining cards need to be put in a stack in the middle.
- Each player checks first how many pairs they have in their own set of cards. Each pair (word + image) needs to be taken out of the game. (E.g.: Player A has 1 pair, player B has 2 pairs, and players C and D do not have any)

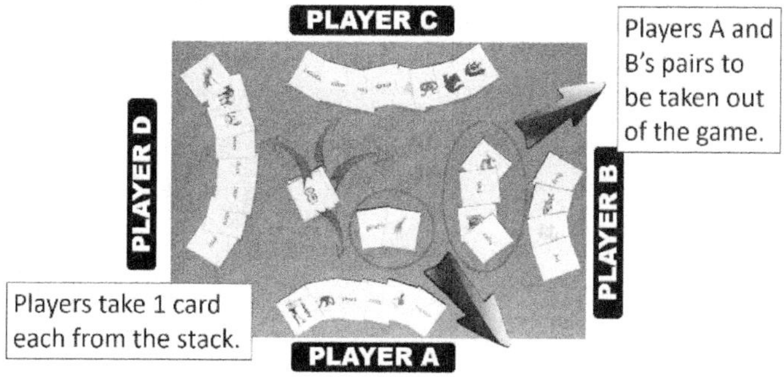

- Once all the pairs are removed, in turn, each player picks one card from the stack. If it makes up a pair, the player removes it from the game. If not, they need to keep the card.
- Once all the cards from the stack have been picked, in turn, each player picks randomly a card from the player on their left. Each time it makes a pair, the player removes it. The number cards each player holds reduces little by little.
- The player who gets rid of all their cards wins!
- As the joker is the only card without a pair, it will stay in the game until the end. The loser is the player who ends up with the joker.

<u>**Learning process and why it works:**</u>

- The players need to read the words on the cards in order to be able to match them to the corresponding images.

<u>**Variations**</u>:

- For beginner readers, keep the number of cards in the game the same, but only hand out 6 cards to each player to start with. The rest will be put in a stack in the middle.

Support:

- Have a help sheet accessible. This could be a sheet you previously used to explain how to read a letter in certain contexts, or have the words written under the pictures representing them. Let your child have access to the material they previously used to learn them. **The retrieval process**[35] your child will be going through will reinforce the learning each time.

[35] See glossary at the back for an explanation (p222-226).

#18 Flip the Board

Preparation time:	Minimum level of mastery of the language required
🕐	☆/ 📖📖
Minimum number of participants: 2	**Material required**: Mini whiteboard or A5 paper Whiteboard pen or Felt-tip pen
Aim of the activity: To recognise the overall shape of a word. This will help your child read faster over time.	

Preparation of the resources:

- Write a word on a mini whiteboard (or on A5 sheets of paper). Make sure you write them in lower case so that the shape of the word is more visible (as explained in chapter 2 - *How to start teaching a language with the same writing system to the one your child knows already*)
- If you use A5 sheets, prepare a minimum of 5 cards, and a maximum of 15 so that you can review the words several times.

Instructions for the activity:

- ① You hold the mini whiteboard (or the sheets of paper) words against your chest.
- ② You flip the card / mini whiteboard quickly to only give a chance to your child to have a glimpse of the word/character.
- Your child needs to say the word out loud.
- Adapt the speed at which you flip a card to the level of proficiency of your child.

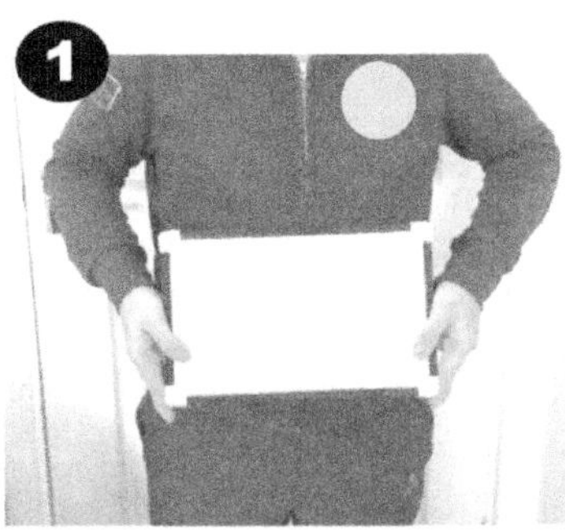

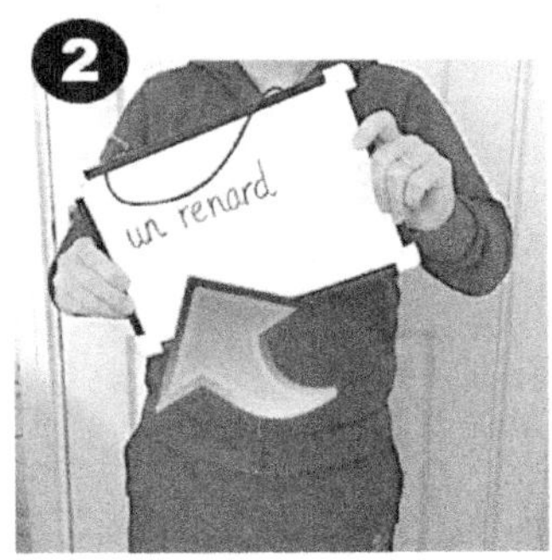

Learning process and why it works:

- The speed of this game helps your child get familiar with the overall shape of the word/character presented.
- Your child will spot a few details of the words and will work out the others from the overall shape. This will therefore help your child recognise and read the words faster.

Variations:

Support:

- Give the list of words you are going to be flipping, or an extensive list of words from which you picked the words you wrote on the cards. Give a chance to your child to go through the list before starting the activity.
- Alternatively, you can also tell the type of words you wrote (e.g.: animals, objects in the house, etc.). The aim is to provide a direction.

Challenge!

- Write longer words.

#19 Rolling Words

Preparation time: ⌚⌚	Minimum level of mastery of the language required ☆/ 📖📖
Minimum number of participants: 2	**Material required**: Ping-pong balls Whiteboard marker Cardboard Mini whiteboard
Aim of the activity: Recognition of letters/words.	

Preparation of the resources:

- Write one letter per ping-pong ball. All the letters together form a word. (You can write the letter several times on the ping-pong ball so that your child has more chances to spot it when rolling)
- With cardboard, create a 50cm slightly inclined ramp for the ping pong balls to roll in a straight line.

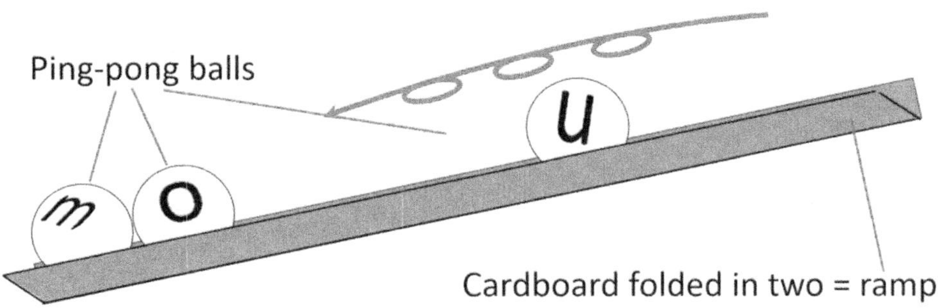

Instructions for the activity:

- Roll the balls one at a time, in the order the word is spelled.
- Your child needs to read the letter on the ball rolling (roll it as many times as needed).
- They write it on a mini whiteboard or a piece of paper.
- The aim is to guess the word before all the letters are rolled.

Learning process and why it works:

- Your child will discover the letters one by one in a fun way.
- By deciphering the word one letter at a time, your child will be reproducing the reading steps (recognising, sounding out and blending the letters together).

Variations:

Support:

- Make sure the ball rolls in a straight line, and roll it slowly.
- Before starting the game, tell your child how many letters there are in your word. They can write a dash for each letter on the mini whiteboard / piece of paper. While writing the letters out one by one, your child can work out the word based on the letters they have already discovered and the total number of letters.
- You can have a topic such as "animals", "places", etc. This will guide your child.

Challenge!

- Use a tray instead of a ramp for the ball to roll in every direction. The letter therefore will not necessarily appear the right way up.

#20 The Word Train

Preparation time: ⏲⏲ (No preparation time needed if you already have the cards)	**Minimum level of mastery of the language required** ☆☆/ 🕮🕮
Minimum number of participants: 2 (See the "variations" section for a 1 player game option)	**Material required**: 1 set of word cards (create your own or find downloadable sets on www.library4multilinguals.com)
Aim of the activity: Analysing the words, reinforcing knowledge of spelling.	

Preparation of the resources:

- You need a set of word cards: 10 cards per player + 10 in the stack. (E.g.: for 2 players, you will need 30 cards)
- Write a list of possible common points between the cards (see below for examples)

Examples of common points:

Both words start/end with the same letter/sound.

Both words have silent letters.

Both words contain the same sound (spelled similarly or differently).

Both words have the same number of letters.

Both words have a prefix/suffix[36].

Both words are homophones[37] (Can be a pair of homophones, or the fact that they each have a homophone).

Both words are cognates[38].

Both words are false friends[39].

---

[36] See glossary at the back for an explanation (p222-226).
[37] See glossary at the back for an explanation (p222-226).
[38] See glossary at the back for an explanation (p222-226).
[39] See glossary at the back for an explanation (p222-226).

Both have similar radical / prefix / suffix (or similar component in the case of Chinese characters).

Instructions for the activity:

- Give between 5 and 10 cards to each player and have 10+ cards in the stack. Note that younger players will find it easier to analyse fewer words.
- The youngest player puts a word card down.
- Going around clockwise, the next player puts on either side of the card (left or right) another card. This card needs to have at least one common point mentioned in the list. The cards appear like the wagons of a train linked to each other.
- If the player cannot put down any card, they need to pick one card from the stack. If they can put the card down, they do it. Otherwise, they keep it and the next person plays.
- The player who gets rid of all their cards wins.

- Optional rule: For each common point found, the player scores 1 point. The player with the most points wins.

Example in English

Possible common points:
- They both have the prefix or suffix.
- They both have the same radical.

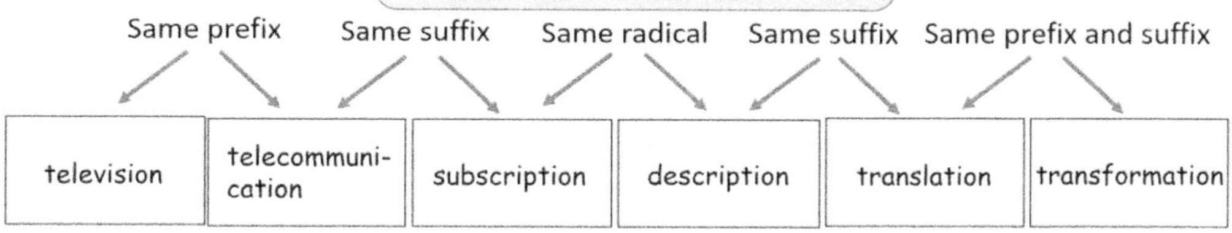

Example in Korean

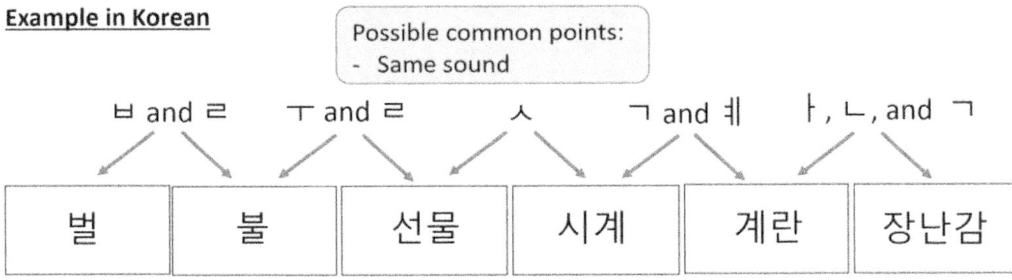

Learning process and why it works:

- By analysing the words, your child will start learning more and more about how the words are formed. This will contribute to consolidating your child's spelling as well.
- The game aspect of it will make analysing words an enjoyable process.

Variations:

- **Game for 1 player:** your child has all the cards and needs to get rid of all of them by stating a common point.

Support:

- Every player has their cards down on the table, visible to everyone, so that players with better knowledge of the language can help others. This will encourage your child to not only find common points with the words on each end of the word train, but with those that different players have. It then becomes a cooperative game where players collaborate to attach all their words to the "word train" in a tactical way.

Challenge!

- Include new words that your child is not familiar with, and help them work out the meaning. E.g.: if you are working on prefixes and suffixes[40], let your child work out the meaning.

[40] See glossary at the back for an explanation (p222-226).

#21 The Odd One Out

Preparation time: 🕒	**Minimum level of mastery of the language required** ☆☆/ 📖📖
Minimum number of participants: 2	**Material required**: Mini whiteboard or paper Pen
Aim of the activity: Analysing the details of words to understand their different components (sounds, letters, graphemes[41], etc.)	

<u>**Instructions for the activity:**</u>

- On a mini whiteboard or sheet of paper, write three words.
- Ask your child which one is the odd one out, and to explain.
- There can be (should be) more than one possible answer. The aim is to let your child find common points and differences between the words written. Encourage your child to analyse the meaning of the words, the spelling, the sounds, etc.

  E.g. : fox – elephant – cat
  - "Fox" is the odd one out because "elephant" and "cat" both end with a "t" but not "fox".
  - "Elephant" is the odd one out because both "cat" and "fox" have three letters, but "elephant" has more.
  - "Cat" is the odd one out because both "elephant" and "fox" contain the sound [f] although not spelled in the same way. (This can be a way to teach your child about the different ways the sound [f] can be spelled.
  - "Elephant" is the odd one out, because it is the only one starting with a vowel.
  - "Elephant" is the odd one out, because it is the only herbivore.
  - Etc.

[41] See glossary at the back for an explanation (p222-226).

Learning process and why it works:

- This game encourages your child to analyse and focus on as many details as possible. As a consequence, this activity will help your child's spelling.

Variations:

Support:

- To start with, guiding your child towards particular points will help. You can for example focus on the common / different phonemes[42] and graphemes.

Challenge!

- Write two words and ask your child to write a third word that has common points with both. E.g.: You write "elephant – fox". Your child could write "fire" and explain that the common point is the sound [f]. The sound [f] is spelled "f" and "ph". The focus on the sound is an opportunity to reinforce the different graphemes of the same sound. If your child does not spell the word properly, this is an opportunity to teach/remind them.

[42] See glossary at the back for an explanation (p222-226).

#22 Unjumble the Words

Preparation time: 🕐	**Minimum level of mastery of the language required** ☆☆/ 🕮🕮
Minimum number of participants: 1	**Material required**: Pen Paper
Aim of the activity: Improving spelling	

Preparation of the resources:

- This is a "zero preparation needed" game.

Instructions for the activity:

- Decide on a category with your child. E.g.: animals, places to go, countries, toys, etc.
- Write a word by mixing all the letters.
- Your child needs to guess what it is.
- Then swap the roles.

E.g.: Category = vehicle.

Language	Jumbled up letters	Answer	Notes
French	o u t r v i e u e n	une voiture	In French, you can include the article (un/une) to reinforce the gender of a noun (masculine/feminine)
English	a r c	car	If the word is very short, you can add an adjective and an article[43] e.g. "a small car". Then mention how many words there are.
Japanese	まくる	くるま	You can then ask your child to write it in *kanji*[44] (車)
Korean	ㅇ ㄷ ㅊ ㅈ ㅏ ㅏ ㅗ	자동차	You can separate all the letters for your child to combine them together.

[43] See glossary at the back for an explanation (p222-226).
[44] See glossary at the back for an explanation (p222-226).

<u>**Learning process and why it works:**</u>

- The category you decide makes your child think of different words they know. They then mentally match them with the letters on the paper.
- This exercise helps revise the spelling of words as all the letters needed are present.
- This exercise reinforces the knowledge of silent letters and various combinations of letters (graphemes[45]).

<u>**Variations**</u>:

Support:

- You can keep the letters forming a grapheme together. E.g.: by writing "**p h** e t e l **a n**" it is easier to work out the word "elephant" than if you present the letters in the order "e n a e t l h p".
- Instead of a category, you can have images or real-life objects to illustrate the jumbled-up word. Your child will therefore know straight away what the word is and will only need to work out the order of the letters.

Challenge!

- You can write a long word and try to make as many words as possible with its letters.

[45] See glossary at the back for an explanation (p222-226).

#23 Can you Read this Word?

Preparation time:	**Minimum level of mastery of the language required**
⏱	☆☆☆/ 📖📖
Minimum number of participants: 1	**Material required**: Pen Paper
Aim of the activity: Spelling (only for languages with deep orthography[46] – languages where a sound/phoneme[47] can be written in different ways, or contain silent letters)	

Preparation of the resources:

- Use different graphemes[48] of a phoneme to write a word.
  E.g.: "Fish" could be spelled "ghos" → "gh" = [f] (as in "enough"); "o" = [i] (as in "women") ; "s" = [ʃ] (as in "sugar").
  In French, "un coq" (a rooster) could be spelled "ein cheauc" → "ein" = [ɛ̃] (as in "peinture" (paint)); "eau" = [o] (as in "l'eau" (water)) ; "ch" = [k] (as in "orchestre").

Instructions for the activity:

- Write a few words and ask your child to work out the word you meant to write.
- Ask your child to give an example for each part of the word as in the example above.

Learning process and why it works:

- By seeing these letter combinations in different contexts, it will draw your child's attention to the spelling difficulties of some words, and it will

---

[46] See glossary at the back for an explanation (p222-226).
[47] See glossary at the back for an explanation (p222-226).
[48] See glossary at the back for an explanation (p222-226).

remind them of the specificities of certain words (e.g.: "ch" read [k] in "orchestra").

<u>Variations</u>:

Support:

- Only change one or two graphemes (i.e. letter(s) representing a sound) in the word so that it is recognisable. In the example above, you could write for example "fosh". This makes it quite recognisable. You then ask in which word "o" is pronounced [i].

Challenge!

- Brainstorm every word you know that has similar graphemes. E.g.: all the words that contain the sound [z] spelled "s".

#24 Calligraphy

Preparation time:	Minimum level of mastery of the language required
	/
Minimum number of participants: 1	**Material required**: Pen / Felt-tip pen / Brush + paint Paper
Aim of the activity: Focusing on the beauty of "perfectly" formed letters. The aim here is not for you to be the example (unless you can), but more to engage in a conversation around writing. It can be a nice way to refer to the written language, especially when your child is starting to learn to write in a new language and/or if you are introducing a new script.	

Preparation of the resources:

- Depending on the age and interest of your child, search for examples on the internet (examples of words and messages, but also an alphabet chart). There are also plenty of videos and tutorials on YouTube that can guide you and your child.

Instructions for the activity:

- Present the activity as a little project. It can be to write a message beautifully that you then want to frame and display in your house, or to send a hand-written letter to someone special.

Learning process and why it works:

- The aim of this activity is to help your child focus on the aesthetic aspect of writing, to see the beauty in the script they are learning.
- The aim is to emulate positive feelings towards the written language. Choose a nice positive message, then put the calligraphy in a frame to display in your house for your child to be proud of their accomplishment.
- Using different tools such as a fountain pen or a brush will likely make the experience feel special. This should encourage your child to apply themself to the task.

Variations:

Support:

- Have examples to copy. Draw lines to help your child keep letters/characters in line and proportionate.

Challenge!

- Let your child choose their own word or message to write.

#25 Word Illustrations

Preparation time:	Minimum level of mastery of the language required
🕐	☆/ 📖
Minimum number of participants: 1	**Material required**: Paint / felt-tip pens Paper
Aim of the activity: Playing on the shapes of the letters to practise writing in an artistic way.	

Preparation of the resources:

- Create a face using different letters or characters.
- In Japan, the most famous face created with letters uses the letters へのへのもへじ.

Here are a variety of shapes you can create:

Human face with the letters へのへのもへじ	Cat with the same letters へのへのもへじ	Dog with the letters へへいしのへのも

Instructions for the activity:

- First show a couple of examples you have created and ask your child to spot all the letters.
- Then let your child's imagination go wild and create a piece of art only using letters or characters!!

Learning process and why it works:

- Your child will get more familiar with the shapes of the letters, in a fun way.
- The added bonus of this activity is that the letters do not need to be perfectly formed. They can only be recognisable, as long as they make up a drawing.

Variations:

Support:

- Have an alphabet chart for your child to refer to it.

Challenge!

- Write a long word and see what drawing you can create with its letters.

#26 Puzzle Words

Preparation time:	Minimum level of mastery of the language required
Minimum number of participants: 1	**Material required**: Cardboard / thick paper (minimum size: 10cm x 10cm) Felt-tip pen / marker pen Cutter / scissors Optional: patterned gift wrap, paint.
Aim of the activity: Paying attention to details of the shape of letters/characters.	

Preparation of the resources:

- On a piece of cardboard or thick paper, write a word or a letter that takes the entire space.
- With a cutter or scissors cut the word or letter in small pieces.
- Prepare a model of the letter or word on a separate piece of paper.

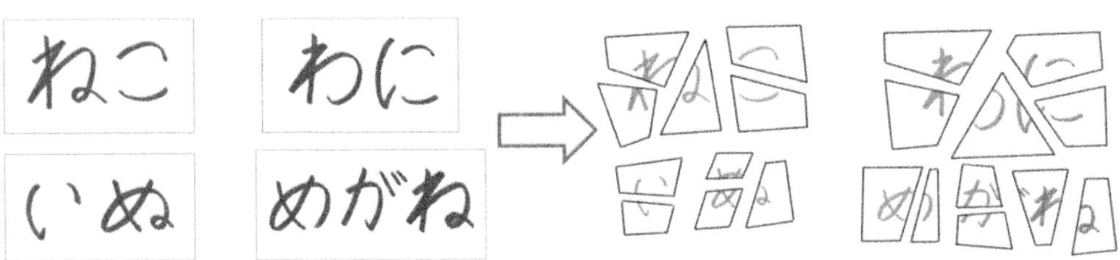

Instructions for the activity:

- Your child needs to look at the model and reconstitute the word / letter.

Learning process and why it works:

- The aim is to draw your child's attention to the details of the letter or word. In order to help them write them.

<u>Variations</u>:

Support:

- If you want to create several puzzles that you want your child to use at the same time, you can paint the back of the different puzzles with a different colour.
- You can stick gift wrap on the cardboard and write the word or letter on top. The patterns will help your child orient the pieces in the right direction.

Challenge!

- Add extra pieces to the puzzle that do not belong, in order to focus on the differences, you want to draw your child's attention to. E.g.: in Japanese, ね, れ, わ look very similar. You might want to add an extra piece that will help your child to focus on the details differentiating the different characters.

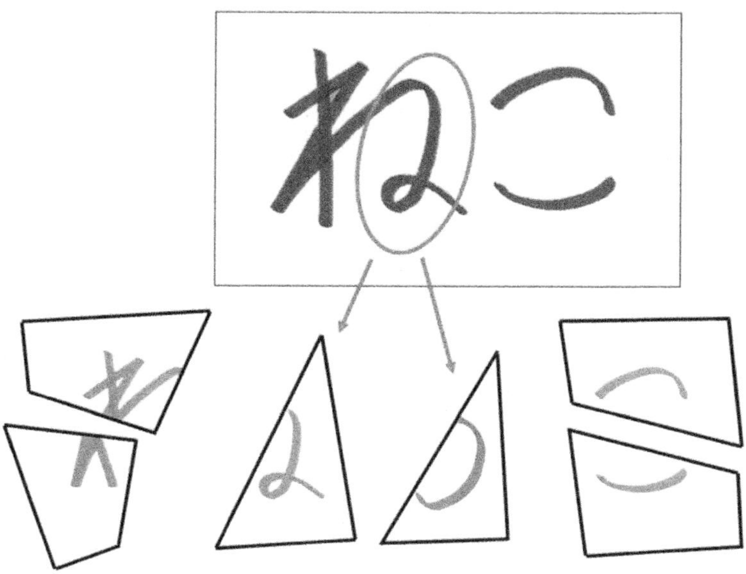

#27 Chopped off Words

Preparation time:	**Minimum level of mastery of the language required**
Minimum number of participants: 1	**Material required**: Pen Paper Scissors
Aim of the activity: Recognition of the shape of letters / characters to support writing accuracy.	

<u>**Preparation of the resources** (see next page for an example):</u>

- Decide on a topic (e.g.: activities outdoors, sports, animals, countries, etc.)
- On a piece of paper, write several words. Cut them in half horizontally.
- Keep the bottom half as it is. Cut the top half to separate the letters.

<u>**Instructions for the activity:**</u>

- Give your child the sheet with the bottom halves and the different top halves of letters.
- Tell your child the topic all the words relate to.
- Your child needs to reconstitute the words by finding the top parts of the letters and placing them correctly. Your child will have to work out the top half of the letters based on the bottom halves. (In the example, from top to bottom, you have the words "crocodile", "ostrich", "caterpillar", and "dinosaur").

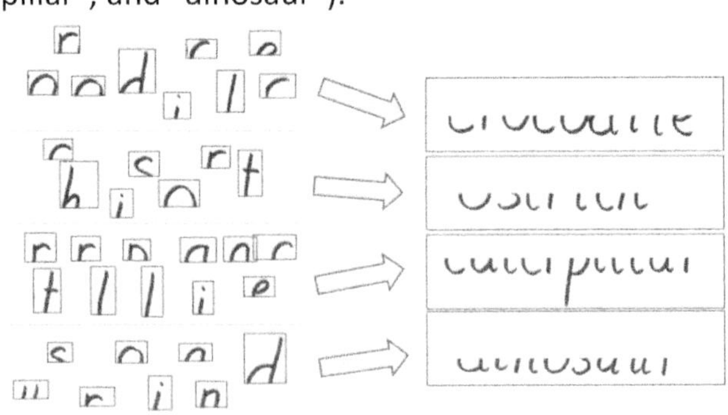

Learning process and why it works:

- In the early stages of learning to read and write, it is important to draw attention to details that need to be remembered to then write accurately.
- This activity makes your child work on their memory of the shapes of letters. Visible clues (i.e. the bottom half of words) guide your child to remember the missing part of the letter.
- The bottom half of the letters *"a"* and *"u"* are similar. *"i"*, *"t"*, and *"l"* can also look very similar. Therefore, if you separate the top half of letters, your child will have to also rely on the other letters that are less ambiguous (e.g. *"s"*, *"f"*). This helps your child retrieve from memory the words they know based on the letters they managed to work out.

Variations:

Support:

- Instead of a broad topic, provide pictures representing the word your child needs to reconstitute.
- Instead of separating the top part of the letters, keep them together so that your child only needs to find the corresponding top half, to read the word. You child will mainly look at the length of the chopped-off part to match them, and read them after.

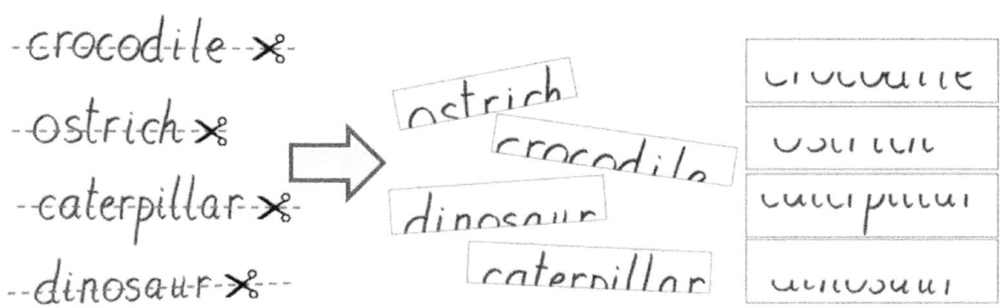

- In languages using the Latin alphabet, the top half of letters are more specific than the bottom half. You can therefore provide the top part and ask your child to reconstitute the bottom part.

Challenge!

- Do not provide the pieces that make up the top half of words. Ask your child to complete the letters by writing them. An alphabet chart can be provided to help your child analyse the shape of the visible parts of the letters. (Please keep in mind that the shape of some letters such as "a" can change depending on the font used. Make sure the shape of letters in the alphabet chart matches the letters you write/type)

- Cut the top halves of letters in an oval shape so that they cannot be placed only by piecing together the papers according to their shapes.

- If you want to work on similar looking letters, present words with these letters E.g. るろ (Japanese). Either give one word containing both letters, or a few words.

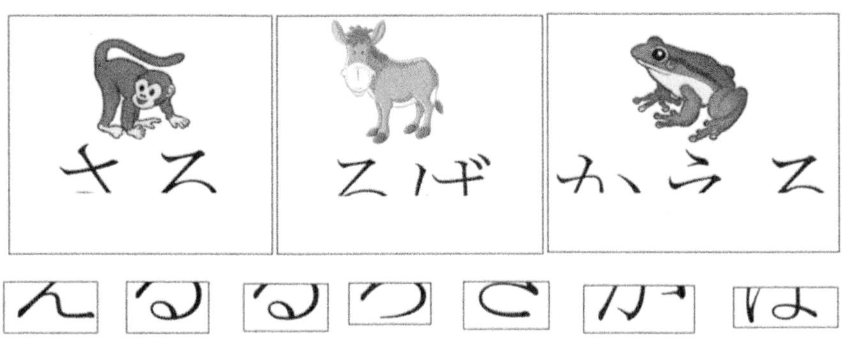

(Monkey = さる; Donkey = ろば; Frog = かえる)

#28 Hangman

Preparation time:	Minimum level of mastery of the language required
Minimum number of participants: 2	**Material required**: Pen Paper
Aim of the activity: Spelling - This activity is especially useful to reinforce the spelling of words that your child is not comfortable with yet.	

Instructions for the activity:

- On a piece of paper, write dashes for each letter in the word you have in mind.
- Your child says different letters of the alphabet.
- If the letter said is part of the word, you write it as many times as it appears in the word. If it is not part of the word, you need to write the letter on the side, and draw a line. All the lines combined will end up representing a man hung.
- Your child needs to find the word before the man is hung.

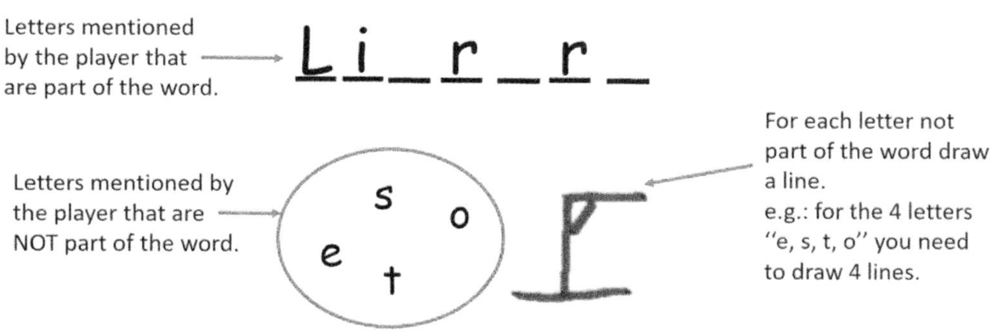

Steps to draw the hangman:

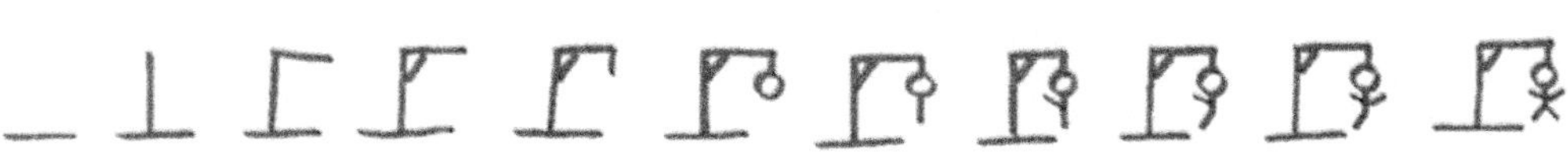

- Ask your child to read the word.

- Optional: you can ask your child to say a sentence containing the word. This is an especially helpful step if the word is a homophone[49], or if you are not sure your child knows its meaning.
- You can then reverse the roles and ask your child to choose a word that you need to guess (see possible support below)

NOTES:

- It is a good idea to have a specific spelling point you want your child to practise (E.g.: a grapheme[50], a phoneme[51], silent letters, pronunciation of some letters in different contexts).
- For languages such as Korean, where the letters do not necessarily follow each other in one direction, you can still present them horizontally. Your child then needs to place the letters appropriately. See example below:

ㄷ ㅏ ㄹ ㅏ ㅁ ㅈ ㅜ ㅣ → 다람쥐

- If a language has different writing systems such as Japanese that has *hiragana*[52], *katakana*, and *kanji*[53], you can use the one most appropriate for this game (*hiragana*, or *katakana* in the example of Japanese). Additionally, if your child can read one but not the other(s), you can use the opportunity to practise the latter.
- In Japanese, for example, *hiragana* is a syllabic writing system that children learn first. Each character represents a syllable. Later on they learn *kanji,* which are Chinese characters (i.e.: ideograms – they convey a meaning). Each *kanji* can be written as *hiragana* (as their main function is to transcribe sound).

  → You could therefore play hangman using *hiragana*, and then ask your child to write the word in *kanji* once they found it.

Learning process and why it works:

---

[49] See glossary at the back for an explanation (p222-226).
[50] See glossary at the back for an explanation (p222-226).
[51] See glossary at the back for an explanation (p222-226).
[52] See glossary at the back for an explanation (p222-226).
[53] See glossary at the back for an explanation (p222-226).

- Your child does not need to know how to spell the word. However, the more letters they guess and see placed in specific positions within the word, the more they are able to work out the whole word by brainstorming the words they know.
- Due to the fact that the words are revealed one letter at a time, your child can consolidate their knowledge of the link between the way words are written and the way they sound.

<u>Variations</u>:

Support:

- Use words that your child has already seen written. You can, for example, restrict yourself to the words that appear in a book you have previously read together.
- When your child writes a word, they can also pick words from a book, in order to be certain of the spelling.

Challenge!

- Say a sentence containing the word found.

#29 Crosswords

Preparation time: ⌚⌚	**Minimum level of mastery of the language required** ☆☆/ 🕮
Minimum number of participants: 1	**Material required**: Pen Internet Printer
Aim of the activity: Spelling - This activity is especially useful to reinforce the spelling of words that your child is not confident with yet.	

Preparation of the resources:

- Decide on a phoneme[54] or grapheme[55] you would like to work on. You can also choose a topic.
- Create a crossword using one of the many crossword generators available online.
- You are generally asked to write the words you want in the grid, and the definition/clue that will help find them. For the clue, you can either write the word in another language your child can read in, write an explanation, or put pictures to represent each word. (You generally cannot place pictures when creating the crossword. However, you can replace the clues by pictures afterwards)

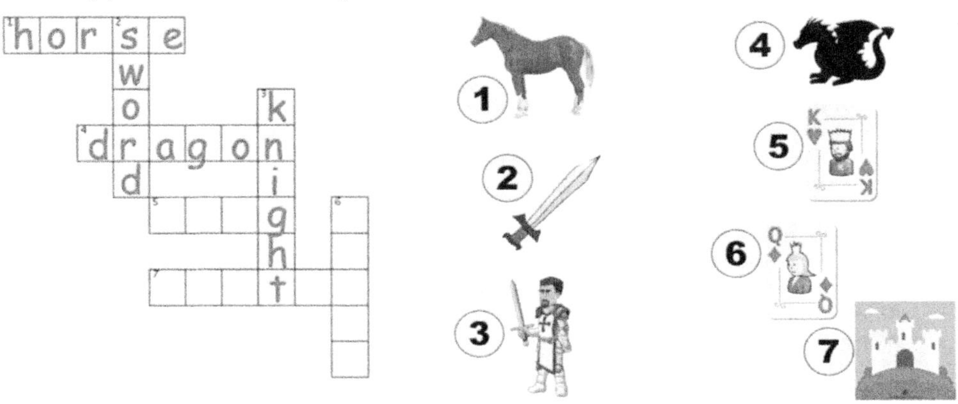

[54] See glossary at the back for an explanation (p222-226).
[55] See glossary at the back for an explanation (p222-226).

Instructions for the activity:

- Your child needs to look at the clues or pictures and write the corresponding word in the grid (as shown in the example on the previous page).

Learning process and why it works:

- Each word has a certain number of boxes. One box can only contain one letter. Two words always have one letter in common. Therefore, for each word, your child knows:
    - Exactly how many letters are required. This can be very helpful with silent letters and double letters.
    - The places of the common letters in two words.

- This allows your child to pay close attention to the spelling of words.

Variations:

Support:

- Use words that your child has already seen written, and do not work on too many complexities at once (i.e.: do not work on too many graphemes or phonemes at once)

Challenge!

- Include new words that your child can work out the spelling based on previous learning.

#30 Artistic Word Analysis

Preparation time: ◷	Minimum level of mastery of the language required ☆☆/ 📖
Minimum number of participants: 1	**Material required**: Pen Paper Optional: paint / felt-tip pens / colouring pencils.
Aim of the activity: Play on the sound of words. This activity enables your child to play with the sound of words, deconstructing and reconstructing them.	

Preparation of the resources:

- Find or draw two or three examples of the following (examples are in English).
  - Choose an animal that is only one syllable long. E.g.: cat, cow.
  - You then need to draw the animal by combining them with the meaning of a longer word containing its name. E.g.: cow → coward, counting, encounter; cat → caterpillar, catastrophic, categorise.

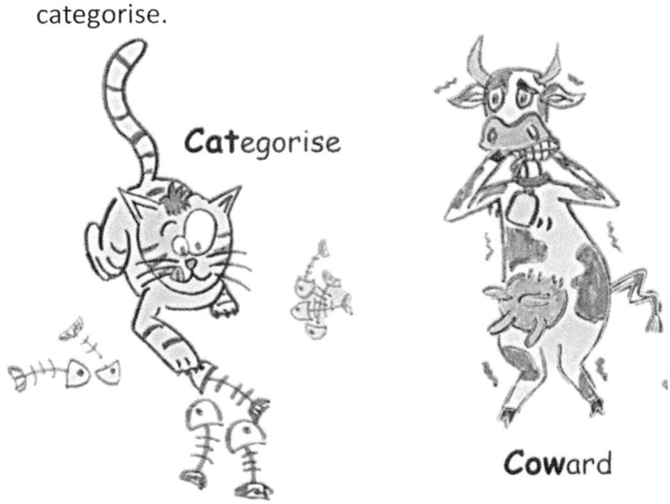

Instructions for the activity:

- Show examples to your child.
- Choose the name of an animal in your language.
- With your child, make a list of longer words that contain the animal's name (remember that the spelling can be different)
- Let your child's creativity go wild!

Learning process and why it works:

- This activity is an opportunity to point at the different spelling of a sound/syllable.
- It is a way to focus on the syllables making up a word and to stretch creativity and imagination.

Variations:

Support:

- Provide examples.

Challenge!

- Make a small comic strip combining several words with the name of one animal.

#31 Rebus

Preparation time: ◷	**Minimum level of mastery of the language required** ☆☆/ 📖
Minimum number of participants: 1	**Material required**: Pen Paper
Aim of the activity: To work on homophones[56] and develop creative thinking.	

Preparation of the resources:

- A rebus is a word or sentence written with images based on their sound.
- Create a rebus. Feel free to use the different languages your child knows.

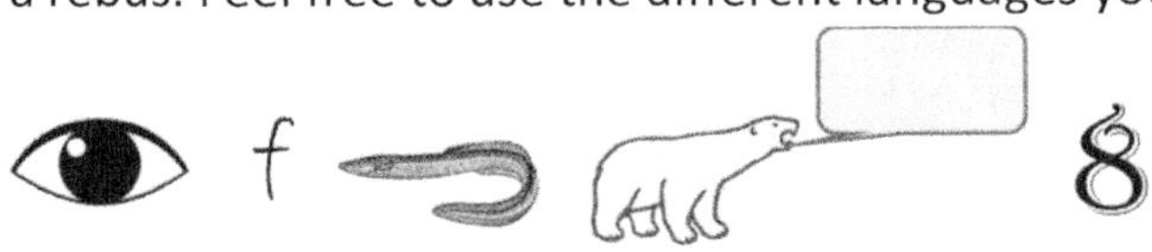

Eye f-eel Grrr eight

Instructions for the activity:

- Your child needs to work out the meaning of the rebus and write it down.
- Once your child has worked out a few of them, let them try to create one.

Learning process and why it works:

- Your child will need to combine the sounds of the words (represented by pictures) to come up with a meaning.
- This is an opportunity to draw attention to the different spelling of sounds and syllables.

Variations:

Support:

- With your child, start creating a chart showing how different syllables can be represented. This will help them create future rebus on their own.

Challenge!

- Create rebus representing a sentence.

[56] See glossary at the back for an explanation (p222-226).

#32 The Word Chain

Preparation time:	**Minimum level of mastery of the language required** ☆☆/
Minimum number of participants: 2	**Material required:** Pen Paper
Aim of the activity: Work on spelling (particularly initial and final syllables/letters)	

Instructions for the activity:

- Player one writes a word down.
- Player two needs to find a word that starts with the last syllable/sound/letter of that word.
- Choose to focus either on the syllables, the sounds, or the letters.
  - ➔ **Syllables**: Only words that contain two syllables or more are allowed. E.g.: football - bowling)
  - ➔ **Sound**: Only words that contain two sounds or more are allowed ("eye" would not be a word you could use as it has only one sound. However, "h-i" or "b-ye" would be accepted). The spelling of the sound can be different. E.g.: "shark" and "sugar" can both follow the word "fish" as they both start with the sound [ʃ].
  - ➔ **Letter**: Only words that contain two letters or more are allowed. E.g.: "enough" can be followed by "history".
- The player who cannot think of a word or repeats a word already written loses.

Note 1: The aim of this game is to help draw your child's attention to the spelling of words. If they can think of appropriate words that fulfil the criteria above, you can help them write them, and take the opportunity to point at the different intricacies there are in the spelling.

Note 2: If in the language used, there are syllables or letters a word cannot start with, the player writing a word ending with that letter loses. E.g.: In Japanese, there are no words starting with ん. If a player says a word ending with it, they are breaking the chain and therefore loses.

Learning process and why it works:

- If done in a collaborative way, this game can offer tremendous opportunities to consolidate your child's spelling and expand their vocabulary.

Variations:

Support:

- When your child cannot think of any word, you can give them clues E.g.: "I know an animal that eats X / lives in X / etc. that starts with the letter …".
- You can also use a dictionary to help you and your child find words that fit the criteria. It is important to use an age-appropriate dictionary.

Challenge!

- Whenever a word is written, an example sentence needs to be said for the word to be put in context. This is especially helpful in case of homophones[57].

---

[57] See glossary at the back for an explanation (p222-226).

#33 Jumble Unjumble (with Jenga)

Preparation time: ◷◷	Minimum level of mastery of the language required ☆☆☆/ 📖📖
Minimum number of participants: 2	**Material required**: Pen Paper Jenga game (Optional) Post-it notes
Aim of the activity: Spelling and expanding vocabulary.	

Preparation of the resources:

- On three of the pieces of the Jenga game, write long words (8 letters or more). You can write them on paper and stick them to the pieces. (This will enable you to change the words every time you play)
- On the other pieces write two letters. One letter on each of the two opposite sides visible when the tower is built (i.e. the two smallest side of the cuboid). You can either write directly on the wooden bricks or, write the letters first on paper or post-it notes, and then tape them to the Jenga piece.
- Once you build the Jenga tower, the three wooden bricks with the words are put at the top. The words on the top pieces should not be visible. All the letters on the other pieces should be visible to the players.

Note: Variation for Chinese characters: Instead of letters, write the different components of characters. One element needs to be a radical[58] (e.g.: 亻, 土, 糹, 氵, etc.)

Instructions for the activity:

- Each player randomly picks a word at the top of the tower. E.g. : cinematography.

[58] See glossary at the back for an explanation (p222-226).

- With the letters of the word, form as many words as possible. Each letter can only be used once. E.g.: cinema, graphic, man, mine, mat, time, etc.
- 1 word = 1 point
- Once the players cannot find any more words, they remove one of the Jenga pieces from the tower. With the two additional letters they get, they need to make again as many words as possible (and add more points to their score). E.g.: The Jenga piece contains "u" and "t". Possible new words are: to**u**r, a**u**toma**t**ic, tr**u**e, tr**ut**h, tro**ut**, etc.
- Note: The piece can (but does not need to) be put back on top of the Jenga tower.

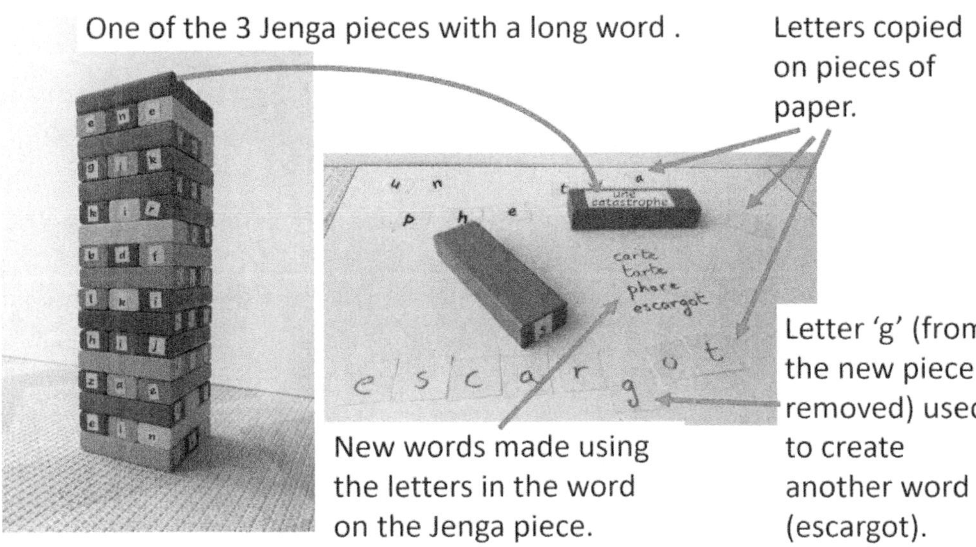

Who wins? The player with the most points wins.

Who loses? The player who topples the tower over loses.

➔ There can therefore be two winners per game: one for the score, i.e. number of words found, and one for not toppling the tower over.

Learning process and why it works:

- This game allows the players to brainstorm words they know while working on the spelling.

Variations:

Support:

- Once the Jenga bricks are removed from the tower, you/your child can copy the letters on small pieces of paper in order to manipulate the letters to move them around.
- You can allow words in different languages.

Challenge!

- Only one letter per Jenga brick. In that case, write the two letters in different colours (e.g.: black and red) and decide at the start of the game which colour can be used by the player with the best knowledge of vocabulary.
- At the end of the game, make up to three sentences containing as many words you found as possible.

#34 The Time Capsule

Preparation time: ⏲	**Minimum level of mastery of the language required** ☆/ 📖
Minimum number of participants: 1	**Material required**: Box Padlock (optional) Paper + Pen
Aim of the activity: Showing progress. From one day to the next, your child might not realise the progress they are making. This activity captures pieces of writing to be rediscovered at a later date.	

Instructions for the activity:

- Find a box and a padlock.
- Collect a few recent pieces of writing representing how much your child can write.
- Put everything in the box, padlock it.
- Explain to your child that you will open it only at a later date to see how much progress they have made. Then decide on a time when you will open the box together. This must be at least a few months in the future. It can be on your child's birthday for example.
- When you open it, let your child discover again what they wrote, and point at the progress you/they can notice. The handwriting might be neater, there might be mistakes they do not do anymore. The aim is to let your child notice (guided by your comments if necessary) the progress they have made. It would be a good idea to mention how the frequent practice led to the improvement they can witness themselves.

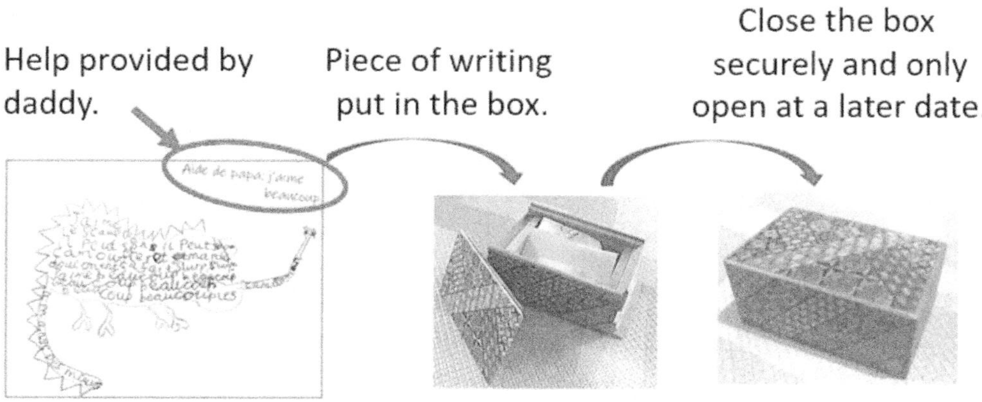

<u>Learning process and why it works:</u>

- Learning to read and write takes a lot of practice, and the progress is not noticeable on a day-to-day basis. By rediscovering old pieces of writing, it should be much more apparent. Your child will be proud, they will build confidence and this exercise should help them understand that little consistent effort pays off.

<u>Variations</u>:

Support:

- Help your child to write and then annotate the piece of writing explaining the help you provided. When you will open the box again, your child might be able to write it without any help.

II) Reading and writing short sentences in a purposeful way.

Between the moment your child can decipher a few words and the moment they can read short stories, there is a big leap. All the building blocks are in place. You "just" need to help your child keep practising. In this section, you will find engaging ways to encourage your child to do so seamlessly, and in an enjoyable way.

One activity that I would highly recommend once your child starts to be able to decipher more or less confidently a few words, is **Puzzle books**! The reason they are perfect for this stage is because the activities are not based on reading. Reading the short instructions enables your child to do the activity. Your child will spend more time doing these fun activities than reading (which at this stage will require a lot of effort). This offers a very good balance between effort and rest/enjoyment.

Typical games you can find in these puzzle books are:

- "Spot the 7 differences between the two pictures."
- Mazes with captions such as "How can the knight reach the tower to free the princess?"
- "Cross the river avoiding X / by repeating the pattern below."
- "Which objects can X take to space?"
- Description: "Find the thief! The thief has a yellow shirt, but he does not wear a hat, ..."

You can see from these examples that all these activities help your child focus on details (and develop their problem-solving skills), which is essential when perfecting reading and writing.

Let us now jump into the variety of activities you can do to help your child practise reading and writing short sentences. Please note that it is recommended that you carry on playing games from the previous section *I) Single letters or words*. Now that your child is more comfortable reading, you just have more activities to help your child enjoy reading and writing.

Reading

#35 Morning Messages

Preparation time:	**Minimum level of mastery of the language required**
Minimum number of participants: 1	**Material required:** Mini whiteboard Whiteboard pen
Aim of the activity: Understanding the meaning of sentences written. Mindfulness: Helping your child start the day positively. When a child lives in a country, the majority language is all around, and reading practice can happen seamlessly. Children can read notices on the bus, games at the back of cereal boxes, etc. This activity recreates this seamless practice.	

Preparation of the resources:

- Write a sentence on a mini whiteboard for your child to discover in the morning during breakfast time.

Instructions for the activity:

- You do not need to point at the message for your child to read. You want your child to discover it, and read it on their own. This should not turn into a reading activity your child has first thing in the morning.
- Let your child read it and react to it.

Note: Start with statements that your child only needs to read such as "I love you", "Look at the blue sky! The weather is so nice today". Later on, you can mix in questions to either spark a conversation or to entice your child to write an answer. E.g.: "What did you dream about?", "How many days are there left until your birthday?"

Learning process and why it works:

- This activity presents no pressure at all to your child. They can read the message or not. Therefore, practice happens without anyone realising it.
- The aim is however to make the messages compelling enough so that your child is looking forward to the one you will be leaving the next morning.

Variations:

Support:

- Write messages you know your child will be able to read. If needed, you can, of course, help your child to read it. This is not a moment to test your child's ability.

Challenge!

- Encourage your child to leave you a message as well. If you leave messages that make your child happy, they are likely to want to do the same for you.

#36 The Broken Space Barre

Preparation time: 🕒	Minimum level of mastery of the language required ☆/ 🕮🕮
Minimum number of participants: 1	**Material required**: Word processing software Alternatively: pen and paper
Aim of the activity: Spelling and punctuation.	

<u>**Preparation of the resources:**</u>

- On your phone or computer, write a sentence or two, and remove every space, punctuation, and capital letter.

<u>**Instructions for the activity:**</u>

- Your child needs to add the spaces, punctuation, and capital letters.

Note 1: Write a text about something that is relevant to your child: How the day is going; Any fun plans for an outing; Comment on a book you are currently reading together; etc.

nextweekendisyourbirthdayguesswhatwewillgocamping

⇩

Next weekend is your birthday! Guess what? We will go camping.

Note 2: In languages such as Korean where letters can be combined horizontally and/or vertically, you could separate all of them. This would help your child work on the different rules dictating letter arrangements.

ㄷ ㅏ ㅇ ㅡ ㅁ ㅈ ㅜ ㄱ ㅏ ㄴ ㅣ ㅅ ㅐ ㅇ ㅣ ㄹ ㅇ ㅣ ㅈ ㅣ ㅁ ㅜ
ㅓ ㅎ ㅏ ㄹ ㅈ ㅣ ㅅ ㅐ ㅇ ㄱ ㅏ ㄱ ㅎ ㅐ ㅂ ㅗ ㅏ ㅆ ㅇ ㅓ ㅅ ㅐ ㅇ
ㅇ ㅣ ㄹ ㄱ ㅣ ㄴ ㅕ ㅁ ㅇ ㅡ ㄹ ㅗ ㅋ ㅐ ㅁ ㅍ ㅣ ㅇ ㄱ ㅏ ㅈ ㅏ

다음 주가 니 생일이지? 뭐 할지 생각해 봤어?
생일기념으로 캠핑가자 !

Learning process and why it works:

- As your child will try to recognise the words and separate them, their attention will be drawn to details. Silent letters and tricky spelling will be noticed more.

Variations:

Support:

- Start with one sentence. If you write more, start a new line for each sentence.

Challenge!

- Write a longer text, and do not leave any space between the sentences.

#37 Coloured Sentences

Preparation time:	Minimum level of mastery of the language required
🕒	☆/ 📖📖
Minimum number of participants: 2	**Material required**: Laptop/computer Alternatively: Paper + Felt-tip pens
Aim of the activity: Reading fluency.	

Preparation of the resources:

- On a piece of paper, or on your computer, write between six and ten sentences that contain about ten words each.
- Each sentence is written in a different colour. Note that although your child might already know the colours, writing them gives the opportunity to show how they are spelled.
- Some sentences can start with the same word(s).

L'animal le plus rapide du monde est le guépard. (rose)

L'animal le plus grand du monde est la baleine bleue. (bleu)

L'animal le plus mignon du monde est mon chat. (rouge)

L'animal qui est le plus intelligent est le dauphin. (vert)

L'animal qui a les plus grandes ailes est l'albatros. (violet)

L'animal qui a le plus long cou est la girafe. (orange)

L'animal que j'aime le plus est le koala. (marron)

Instructions for the activity:

- You read one of the sentences.
- Your child needs to identify the sentence you are reading and say its colour before you finish reading it.
- If you finish first, you get a point. If your child says the colour first, they get a point.

- Repeat the process as many times as you wish, by choosing sentences randomly.
- Then you swap the roles. Your child reads, and you say the colour.

Note: Ideally, you want to prepare two or three sets of sentences with similar words. This allows your child to be quite comfortable reading them, without saying them from memory.

Learning process and why it works:

- This game is based on speed of reading i.e. spotting the words read by the parent fast enough, and reading the sentences fluently.
- Your child will start to be able to recognise the general shape of different words, instead of deciphering them letter by letter.

Variations:

Support:

- Practice makes perfect. In order to make sure your child enjoys the activity, adapt to their level and do not read too fast. Your child should feel like it is possible to say the colour before you read the end of the sentence. That way, they will want to play it more, and therefore practise more.

Challenge!

- Every time a word is misread, the other player gets a point.

#38 The Wobbly Bridge

Preparation time:	**Minimum level of mastery of the language required**
Minimum number of participants: 2	**Material required**: Masking tape Marker pen
Aim of the activity: For your child to understand what they are reading.	

<u>**Preparation of the resources:**</u>

- On strips of masking tape, write sentences.
- Write eight to ten sentences on separate strips of tape.
- Place the strips on the floor, parallel to each other, as if they were the different steps of a bridge.

- Each sentence is referring to something your child knows. It could be about the content of a story to check understanding, or about an event that happened recently. The aim is to make sure that your child understands what they read.

- Have about one third to half of the sentences that are correct. The others should be wrong. Depending on what you want your child to work on, they could contain spelling or agreement[59] mistakes, or simply not make sense.

<u>**Instructions for the activity:**</u>

- Tell your child the criteria. Are the sentences / steps to avoid grammatically incorrect? Is the spelling wrong? Are the sentences referring to a story false?
- Your child reads the first sentence <u>out loud</u>.

---

[59] See glossary at the back for an explanation (p222-226).

- If the sentence is correct, they can step on it. It is a "stable step of the bridge".
- If the sentence is wrong, it is a weak step of the bridge. If your child steps on it, it "breaks" and your child loses.
- The aim is to get to the other side of the bridge.

Note: It is important that your child reads the sentences out loud to make sure that they are reading them, and it does not become a guessing game.

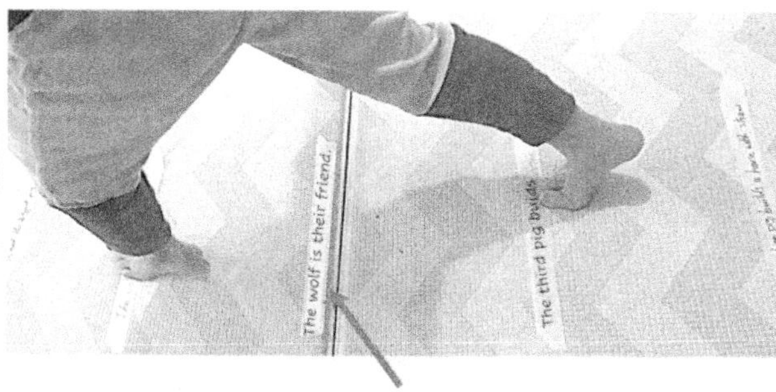

Stepping over a sentence that is wrong.

Optional: If your child reads all the sentences once and manages to get to the other side of the bridge, set a timer. They need to accomplish the same feat in a limited amount of time.

Note: After the first round, your child could think that they know them, and misread some parts. It is therefore important that you set plenty of time on the timer for your child to go back to the start in case they make any mistake. You do not want to set the timer too close to the amount of time your child would need to read the sentences once. (Please, keep in mind that setting a timer is **optional**. If it becomes more frustrating than motivating, do not use one).

Once your child has crossed the bridge in one direction, ask your child to read them starting from the last sentence and cross the bridge in the other direction. (Make sure you turn the sentences around so that your child can stand on the other side of the bridge and read the sentences on each strip).

Learning process and why it works:

- The game should make your child want to read the sentences. In order to make this activity even more compelling, write sentences that can interest your child, or make them laugh.
- Your child does not just need to read, they need to read the words properly in order to understand the meaning of the whole sentences.

Variations:

Support:

- Only use words that you know your child knows and can read.

Challenge!

- Include new words that your child can work out how to read.

- **Variation: Unjumble the text**
    - Each strip is part of a longer text, and the sentences follow each other logically.
    - The strips should not be put in order. Your child needs to read the first sentence and then find the one that follows logically and jump on it.
    - In this case, do not include any mistake. The aim is for your child to step on each sentence in the right order.
    - The closest strip to your child should be the first sentence, and the furthest one is the last one so that even if your child jumps forward and backward, they end up "crossing the bridge".

#39 Catch Me If You Can

Preparation time:	Minimum level of mastery of the language required
◷◷	☆☆/ 📖📖
Minimum number of participants: 2	**Material required**: Post-it notes Pen Counters Dice
Aim of the activity: For your child to understand what they are reading.	

Preparation of the resources:

- Write simple riddles or questions on one side of a post-it note, and the answer at the back.
- Prepare seven post-it notes per player i.e.: if there are two players, you need to prepare fourteen post-it notes.

Instructions for the activity:

- Place them as a circle, on the table. The counters need to be equidistant from each other.
- Roll the dice and move your counter by the number of post-it notes indicated by the dice. You can move the counter either forward or backward.
- You then need to read the question/riddle and answer it. If you answer correctly, you can stay on the post-it note you landed on. Otherwise, you need to go back to the post-it note you were on.
- The aim is to land on the same post-it note as (one of) the other player(s). If you can answer the question/riddle correctly, you catch the other player and win the game!

Note: The longer you play the game, the more chances there are for a riddle or question to have been read already and the answer uncovered. Do not worry if your child says the answer from memory. In order to be able to do this, they still had to recognise the question and read it (at least partially). Your child is therefore practising.

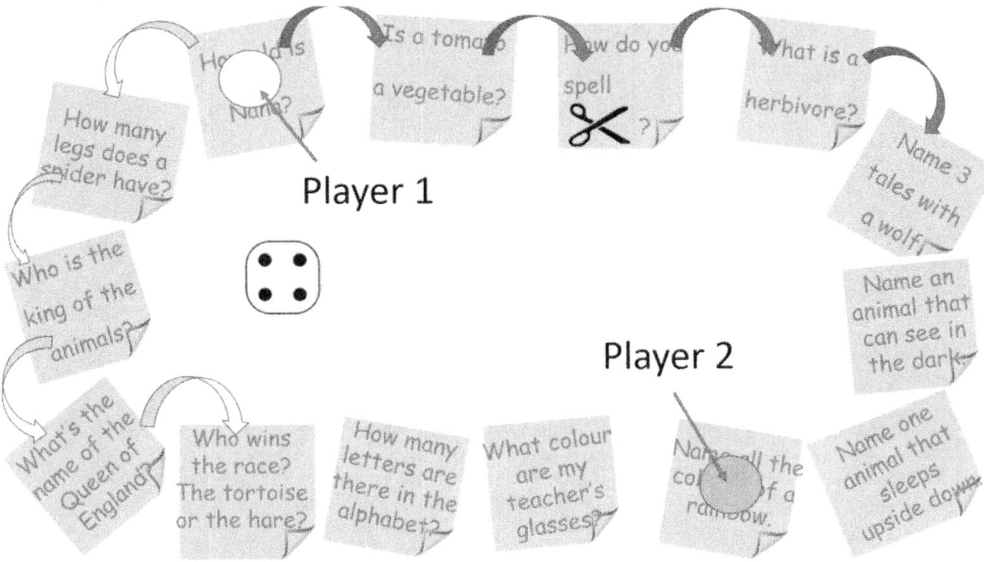

In this example, player 1 rolled a 4. They can move **clockwise** and land on the question "Name 3 tales with a wolf", or **anti-clockwise** and land on the question "Who wins the race? The tortoise or the hare?"

Learning process and why it works:

- Your child will read in a purposeful way. They need to read, understand, and solve the riddle or answer the question correctly in order to have a chance to win. Depending on the level of reading fluency of your child, you can make the riddles, problems, questions, more or less difficult.
- Your child can see the other players read a question/riddle. As they will remember them at least vaguely it will help build confidence when they will be reading them.

Note: This activity can also be a great revision game for your child's school subjects.

Variations:

Support:

- If your child is not comfortable reading yet, help your child to read so that they can then focus on solving the problems or riddles – the fun part of the activity. For children who are just about able to decipher a sentence, you could write simple questions such as "What did we eat for dinner last night?"

Challenge!

- Ask your child to write riddles or problems for you. They could be about facts your child has learnt in school, on TV, in books that you might not know.

#40. 5 Clues 3 guesses

Preparation time:	Minimum level of mastery of the language required
⌚	☆☆/ 📖 📖
Minimum number of participants: 2	**Material required**: Pen Paper Toy box / bag
Aim of the activity: Understanding the meaning of sentences written.	

Preparation of the resources:

- Hide a toy or object in a (toy) box.
- Write five short sentences to describe the hidden object. Write each sentence on a separate piece of paper and fold them.

Instructions for the activity:

- Present to your child the 5 pieces of paper containing the clues.
- Your child can only choose 3 of them randomly.
- They read them and need to guess what the hidden object is.
- Your child can give up to 3 guesses.

Example:

It is brown.
It is soft and fluffy.
It has four legs.
You can use it like a pillow.
It was Santa's present.

Learning process and why it works:

- Your child will not feel intimidated by the length of the sentences.
- The limited choice of clues makes each one very important. Your child will therefore be more motivated to read them and understand them.

<u>**Variations**</u>:

Support:

- Help your child decipher the words if necessary by reminding them of different rules, and referring graphemes[60] to other known words that contain the same ones.
- Your child could read the three clues picked and have one go at guessing what the toy is. If it is wrong, they can pick another one (i.e. read a fourth clue). If it is wrong again, the last clue can be read.

Challenge!

- Write longer and less straightforward sentences.
  E.g.: "It is the same colour as an apple tree in winter" to refer to the colour brown.

---

[60] See glossary at the back for an explanation (p222-226).

#41 Treasure Hunt

Preparation time:	**Minimum level of mastery of the language required** /
Minimum number of participants: 1	**Material required**: Pen Paper Treasure Template available in the RESOURCES PACK to download from www.library4multilinguals.com
Aim of the activity: Reading – The aim is to provide a purpose for reading i.e.: wanting to find the treasure. Understanding the clues and solving the problems and riddles are necessary to reach the goal.	

This game can be played in various ways and be perfectly adapted to your child's needs. Here is one way you could do the treasure hunt activity. See in the *variations* section how to create a simpler version for children who are just starting to feel comfortable reading.

Preparation of the resources:

There are three steps to this treasure hunt:

Step 1: On a sheet, write five or more sentences indicating where the different clues are. E.g.: Check under your pillow; Look inside the piano.	**Step 2**: Solve the riddles or problems that are found in step 1. Each answer gives part of the answer to find out where the treasure is hidden.

1. How do you call the instrument mummy plays so well? Look inside?

2. What book are you reading now? To find a clue, turn to page (7 x 9 = ______)

3. There are four of around the dining table. You sit on one of them. Have a look under it.

Clue number 1: What is the name of this animal?

Clue number 2: What do you need to give to the fairy for her to give you money?

Clue number 3: It is a 3 letter word, and you sleep on it. What is it?

Step 3: Write a coded sentence indicating where the treasure is. For example, this can be a **rebus**[61] or a message written with various shapes.

For a rebus: Each answer from step 2 helps your child read the pictures correctly.

For a message written in codes: A riddle from step 2 could be the name of an animal written in code to get your child to work out part of the code. (see example below for English)

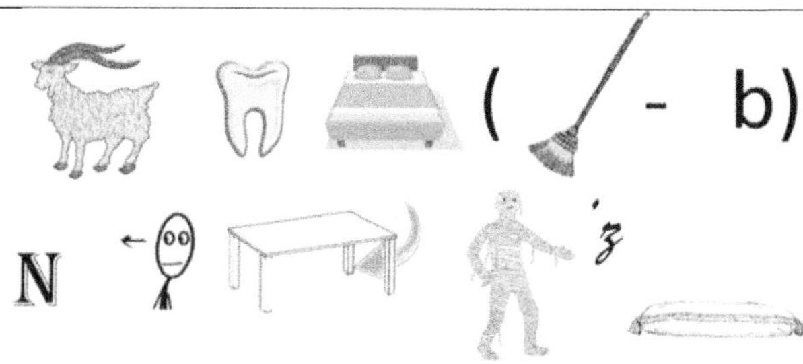

This rebus says: "**Goat tooth bed (broom – b) N look under mummy'z pillow**".
Understand: "**Go to the bedroom and look under mummy's pillow**".

Note: When writing the clues, adapt to your child's ability, and feel free to change languages for each step.

- In step 1, use the language your child is the least confident with, and write very simple sentences. It could even be a single word indicating the location of the clue E.g.: piano, red shoes, under your pillow.
- In step 2, you can write the riddles and problems to solve in the language your child is most comfortable reading.
- In step 3, if you choose to write a rebus, you can use a language your child can only speak but not read or write, as it is based on pictures.

Instructions for the activity:

- Let your child enjoy searching and solving riddles.
- Help your child read if necessary, to understand where the clues are.

[61] See in Chapter 2, the activity ***Rebus*** for clarifications about the activity.

Learning process and why it works:

- This activity gives a high emotional incentive to read. The practice consequently becomes seamless.
- Without understanding the meaning, your child cannot find the clues, and therefore the treasure. It is not only important to be able to decipher the words, but it is crucial to understand their meaning.

Variations:

Support:

- For children only starting to read, you can write different clues that will lead them from one clue to the next, up to the treasure.

E.g.:

Message 1: Check under your pillow.

Message 2: Look inside your red shoes.

Message 3: Look behind the red cushion on the sofa.

Message 4: Find the treasure in your wardrobe.

Challenge!

- Depending on the level of your child, you could make the messages written more difficult - as riddles for example.

E.g.: *It is very soft, and my head would not be at rest without it. What is it?*

Mummy plays this instrument wonderfully. Let's check inside!

#42 Unjumble the sentences

Preparation time:	Minimum level of mastery of the language required
Minimum number of participants: 1	**Material required**: Pen Paper Scissors Optional: photos
Aim of the activity: Order of words. There are many differences between languages and often, the majority language can impact the home language. E.g.: order of words, adjective agreements[62], verb conjugations, etc. This activity aims to help your child notice and learn accurately the syntax and other specificities of the home language.	

Preparation of the resources:

- Write a sentence on a strip of paper.
- Cut the paper to separate the words. (Make sure you cut the paper so that your child cannot just put the sentence back together by assembling the sentence like a puzzle)

Notes:

- All the sentences you write can make up a story that your child will discover little by little, one sentence at a time.
- What grammatical or syntactic aspect of the home language do you want your child to work on? Include it in the sentences. E.g.: If you want to work on the word order of nouns and adjectives, include some in each sentence.
- Do not overwhelm your child by including too many points to work on. Your child is more likely to learn quickly and securely if they only need to think of a few of them.

[62] See glossary at the back for an explanation (p222-226).

petit	petite	petits	cochons	bois.	maison	une
était	dans	fois	Il	trois	qui	une	d'un	tout
vivaient	près

↓

Il	était	une	fois	trois	petits	cochons	qui
vivaient	dans	une	petite	maison	tout	près
d'un	petit	bois.

In French, adjectives agree with the noun they describe. "Petit", "petite", and "petits" (small) are three different ways to describe a noun - respectively masculine singular (un bois), feminine singular (une maison) and masculine plural (trois cochons). By including these variations, your child needs to work out which adjective describes which noun and then match them accordingly.

<u>**Instructions for the activity:**</u>

- Give to your child the pieces/words to make up one sentence.
- Once the sentence is made, let them read it out loud to see if it makes sense.

  Note: By hearing it, your child might be able to spot the mistakes. If they cannot see them, here are a few "non-threatening" ways to help your child correct themself.

  - **Give an alternative:** "Do we say ... or ...?"
  - **Ask questions to model the reasoning:** "If it is written 'three', does it mean there is only one or many? And if it is written 'maison', does it mean there is only one or more? So can we write 'trois maison'?"

Remember that it also took us a long time to be able to speak, read, and write properly. Let's be patient when teaching our children.

Learning process and why it works:

- Having cut out words that your child can manipulate will help them mentally manipulate the words as well.
- This activity helps your child remember, learn, and consolidate a variety of syntactic and grammatical aspects of the home language.

Variations:

Support:

- You can base your sentences on stories your child knows very well. The sense of familiarity will help your child focus emotionally, and they are less likely to think that the task is too difficult.

Challenge!

- You can then add or substitute words to discuss any changes that happen as a consequence.
  E.g.: You work on verbs in the past tense based on *The Three Little Pigs*. The sentence is "The straw house **was** fragile". If you add "and the stick house", you can point at the fact that "was" becomes "were".

#43 Jump and Read

Preparation time: 🕐	Minimum level of mastery of the language required ☆☆/ 🕮🕮
Minimum number of participants: 1	**Material required**: Whiteboard pen Mini whiteboard Trampoline
Aim of the activity: Recognition of the overall shape of the words.	

This activity is ideal for active children!

Instructions for the activity:

- Write a message on the mini whiteboard.
- Place the whiteboard at a height or angle that requires your child to jump on a trampoline to be able to read the sentence.

Note: write sentences that are funny or sweet that your child will want to discover.

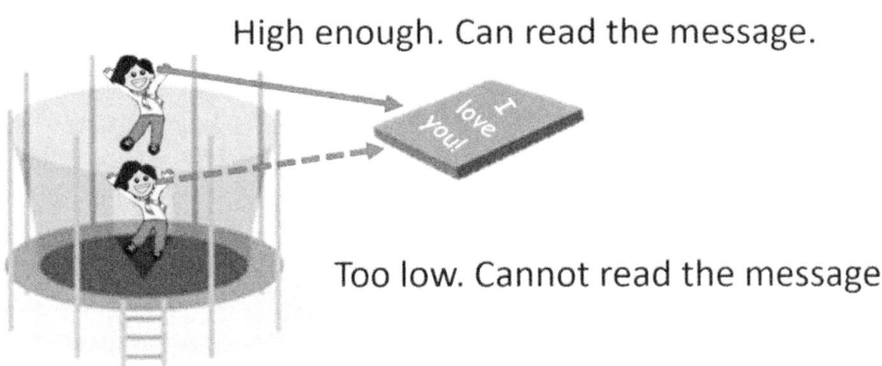

Learning process and why it works:

- Your child will not be able to read everything at once. They will however reconstitute the whole message with the pieces of information collected during the short amount of time available to see your sentence.

- This helps your child associate the overall shape of words with the words they know.

<u>**Variations**</u>:

Support:

- Tell your child the type of thing written on the board. E.g.: an activity you will do later, a joke about animals, etc.

Challenge!

- Limit the number of times your child can jump and peek at the sentence.

#44 Double Messages

Preparation time:	Minimum level of mastery of the language required
🕒	☆☆/ 📖
Minimum number of participants: 1	**Material required**: Notebook Pencil
Aim of the activity: Writing for fun. Engage your child in the writing process by writing opposing, cheeky, surprising messages.	

Preparation of the resources:

Prepare an example:

- Bend the notebook and write a message.
- Bend the notebook the opposite way. You should be able to faintly see the first message. In the same location write a similar message. For best impact it should be a little cheeky or funny.

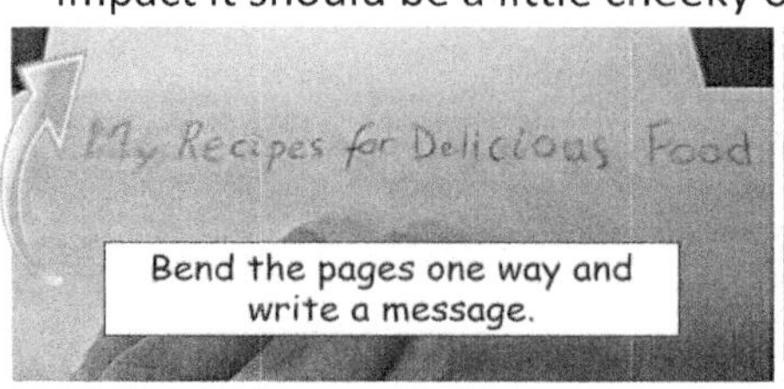

Bend the pages one way and write a message.

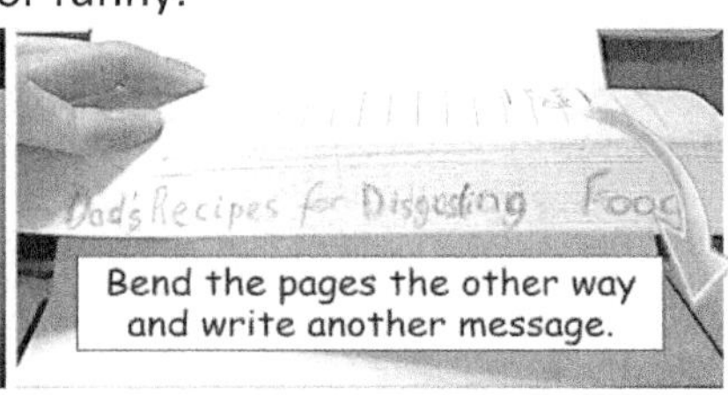

Bend the pages the other way and write another message.

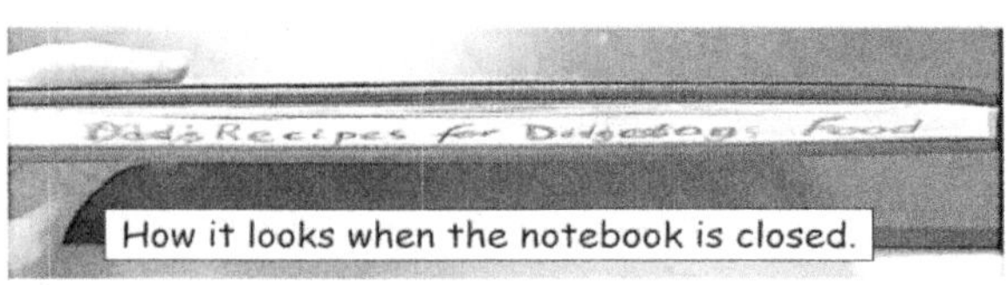
How it looks when the notebook is closed.

Note: When bending the notebook, replace the minimal number of words. In the second sentence, you could write the antonym[63] of a word in the first one.

Here are a few suggestions:

- My recipes for delicious food / Dad's recipes for disgusting food.
- Ideas of a genius kid! / Ideas of a smelly kid!

Instructions for the activity:

- Brainstorm with your child antonyms, or pairs of words with very different meanings, that contain more or less the same number of letters.
- Then come up with fun, interesting, or silly messages to write on the side of a notebook.
- Let your child write them.

Learning process and why it works:

- As you help your child brainstorming words and antonyms, it is an opportunity for them to enrich their vocabulary. The potential impact of the message will make the discovery of new words more memorable.
- The constraints imposed (i.e. the similar number of letters and the fact that the pairs need to have very differing meanings) will help your child expand their vocabulary.

Variations:

Support:

- Use a dictionary of synonyms[64] (Thesaurus).

Challenge!

- This activity could help you and your child create a title for a story (that you could write/draw together – see activity *#71 Ping-Pong Writing*).

[63] See glossary at the back for an explanation (p222-226).
[64] See glossary at the back for an explanation (p222-226).

#45 Create your Own Menu

Preparation time:	**Minimum level of mastery of the language required**
Minimum number of participants: 1	**Material required**: Pen Paper Menu template available in the RESOURCES PACK on www.library4multilinguals.com
Aim of the activity: Reading and copying words.	

Preparation of the resources:

- Plan dishes that can be personalised to individual tastes. E.g.: mini-pizza, sandwich, salad, sushi rolls.
- Create an order sheet with different sections for your child to personalise their food order. The different sections could be:

  On my pizza I want : ____________________________

  Please, remember not to put any : ____________________________

  On the side, I would like: ____________________________

  I would love a glass of: ____________________________

  For dessert, I am going to have: ____________________________
- At the bottom of the order sheet, include the available options.

My order

On my pizza I want : ________________

Please, remember not to put any : ________________

On the side, I would like: ________________

I would love a glass of: ________________

For dessert, I am going to have: ________________

Options

water cake mushroom chilly sauce ketchup cheese crisps nothing tomato sweet corn olives clementine cucumber strawberries chocolate sauce salad orange juice banana milk barbecue sauce hot chocolate ice-cream anchovies

Instructions for the activity:

- Give the order sheet to your child.
- Your child completes the order sheet by reading the available options and copying those desired.
- Return the order to your child if there are mistakes, and explain that you can only prepare a meal if the instructions / the order is clear!
- You prepare the order, and ... *"Bon appétit!!"*

Learning process and why it works:

- Your child will be incentivised by the fact that they can choose whatever they want to eat (and not eat) and will make an effort to understand what the options they have are.
- A child can read more accurately than they can write. By copying, they will become familiar with the spelling of words.

Variations:

Support:

- You keep the different options written at the bottom of the order sheet, but provide a separate sheet with the pictures of all the options. Your child will be able to understand what the options are, and will look for the words corresponding to what they want to eat.
- You can precede this activity by a match-up activity with words on one side, and images on the other side (in a different order than the words). Let/help your child match them up. When you will give the order sheet, it will be easier for your child to spot the food they want.

Challenge!

- If your child can already write confidently, instead of the words written at the bottom to copy, only provide pictures.

#46 Alien Code

Preparation time: ⏲⏲	Minimum level of mastery of the language required ☆/ 📖📖
Minimum number of participants: 1	**Material required**: Pen Paper Optional: word processor and printer
Aim of the activity: Reinforcement of spelling, and focus of various graphemes[65] for one phoneme[66].	

Preparation of the resources:

- Create a code with shapes and colours. Each symbol represents a letter in the language your child is learning to read and write in. And write the letter in your alphabet corresponding to each symbol.
  (Alternatively, you can use a word processor: type the alphabet of your language, select what you wrote, and change the font to "wingdings" or any equivalent that uses symbols)
- Write a short message using this code, and include spelling mistakes.

---

[65] See glossary at the back for an explanation (p222-226).
[66] See glossary at the back for an explanation (p222-226).

Instructions for the activity:

- Explain to your child that this message has been sent to them by an alien.
- Provide the code and its translation.
- Your child might spot already some spelling mistakes when decoding. If there are mistakes that were not spotted, guide them with questions.
  Either be general and help them proofread by targeting specific points. E.g.: "Do you remember that the sound [o] can be spelled in different ways? Let's check if the alien used the right spelling".
  Or point directly at the word containing the mistake and ask "Is that how X is spelled?"
  Or point exactly at the mistake. E.g.: "Oh! I have just spotted another mistake! The alien wrote 'two elephant'. What did he forget to write at the end of 'elephant'?"

Learning process and why it works:

- Breaking the code makes the discovery of the message both fun and challenging.
- Your child learns to proofread by correcting someone else's mistakes. There is therefore less pressure or negative emotions related to mistakes. As you include the type of mistakes they make, your child learns to proofread themself.

Variations:

Support:

- Include a few obvious mistakes so that your child feels more confident by spotting them.
- You can mention how many mistakes the message contains.

Challenge!

- Focus on certain spelling difficulties. E.g.: omit the silent letters, use homophones[67], use the wrong grapheme (e.g.: write "rain" as "rane"). Make sure you only include the type of mistakes your child is making.
- Do not provide any translation for the symbols used. Only provide your child's name written both in code and in the alphabet you are teaching your child. Then, let your child break the code.
  In this case, do not include mistakes as your child will rely on the letters of their name they can place, the number of characters per word, and the repetition of some of them in different words. Decoding such message will be a real detective work and will heavily rely on their knowledge of spelling and grammar, which will consequently be reinforced.

[67] See glossary at the back for an explanation (p222-226).

#47 Distanced Dictation

Preparation time:	**Minimum level of mastery of the language required**
Minimum number of participants: 2	**Material required**: Pen Paper Optional: walkie talkie / home-made phone with 2 pots of yoghurt and a string
Aim of the activity: Reinforcement of spelling.	

Preparation of the resources:

- Write one text with missing parts/information on one sheet, and on another sheet, write the same text, but containing the missing information from the first text, and remove parts that are present in the first text. See example below.

Text A

Il y a _________, j'ai vu une chose incroyable! Une _______ soucoupe volante a atterri dans mon jardin. Et un extraterrestre ______ avec des antennes roses en est sorti. Il était très _______ et ______. Il m'a même raconté une blague!
« Que dit un _________ sur le dos d'une tortue?
_________!! »

Text B

Il y a trois jours, j'ai vu une chose _________! Une petite soucoupe volante a atterri dans mon ______.
Et un extraterrestre violet avec des ________ roses en est sorti. Il était très gentil et drôle. Il m'a même raconté une ________!
« Que dit un escargot sur le dos d'une _________?
Yiiihaaaa!! »

Note: Make your texts something that your child wants to read about. It could be an outing you are planning, or a little story you made up that would resonate with your child, or anything else that would grab your child's attention.

Instructions for the activity:

- You and your child need to be distanced enough so that you cannot read what is on each other's sheet. If you have walkie-talkies, you can be in different rooms. Alternatively, you can sit back-to-back.
- The person who has the first words starts reading (e.g. Text B), and the other one writes what is said to complete their sheet (E.g.: Text A). Each person reads in turn what there is on their sheet.
  Alternatively, both players read together. Whenever a word is missing, the player needs to stay quiet to hear what the other player is reading.
- If one person does not know how to spell a word, they can ask the other person to spell it out.
- The aim is to have both texts identical.

Text A

Il y a trois jours, j'ai vu une chose incroyable! Une petite soucoupe volante a atterri dans mon jardin. Et un extraterrestre violet avec des antennes roses en est sorti. Il était très gentil et drôle. Il m'a même raconté une blague!
« Que dit un escargot sur le dos d'une tortue?
Yiiihaaaa !! »

Text B

Il y a trois jours, j'ai vu une chose incroyable ! Une petite soucoupe volante a atterri dans mon jardin.
Et un extraterrestre violet avec des antennes roses en est sorti. Il était très gentil et drôle. Il m'a même raconté une blague !
« Que dit un escargot sur le dos d'une tortue ?
Yiiihaaa!! »

Learning process and why it works:

- By having a text compelling enough so that your child wants to find out the missing information, your child will pay more attention to the information already present. They will then be more eager to listen to and write the missing information.
  ➔ This activity is therefore first, a reading activity.

- As your child can ask you the spelling of words, they will do so, and it will consolidate their knowledge. You can also ask them: "How do you think it is spelled?" and assist them if needed.
- This activity is also perfect to work on the alphabet (i.e. the name of the letters) in your home language.
- If both players are reading together, the most confident reader will be supporting the least confident one. It is a great activity siblings who have different levels of proficiency could do together.
- If you are preparing this activity for two children, you can remove the words based on what each child needs to be working on.

<u>**Variations**</u>:

Support:

- Only use words your child knows.

Challenge!

- Instead of reading in turns the parts you have, ask questions to obtain the missing information. This will ensure that your child can work out the type of information missing from the context, which is an important skill to develop. Indeed, when reading independently, it will help your child work out the meaning of new words.
  At first, your child might require help to formulate a variety of questions depending on the information missing.
- Before starting the activity, ask your child to guess / work out the missing words and to write them down. The aim is not to get the exact word. It is for your child to gather clues from the text and use their knowledge of the grammar and sentence structures of the language to find an appropriate word.
  For example, in the sentence *"A flying saucer landed in my________"*, the missing word could be "garden", "school", or any appropriate place. However, it could not be a verb for example.

#48 Mirror Writing

Preparation time: ⌚⌚	**Minimum level of mastery of the language required** ☆/ 📖📖
Minimum number of participants: 1	**Material required**: Pen Pencil Paper Printer
Aim of the activity: Reinforcement of spelling.	

Preparation of the resources:

- Find a comic strip.
- Take a first picture of a frame of it (**a**). Using a simple photo editing software, erase the text (**b**) (alternatively, cut out the speech bubbles once printed).
- Take a second picture of the same frame with the selfie mode on your phone, so that it appears as in a mirror (**c**).
- Print out the first photo of the frame without the text (**b**).

Instructions for the activity:

- Your child looks at the picture taken with the selfie mode (**c**) and tries to copy the text the right way around on **b**.

Learning process and why it works:

- By looking at a text, flipped around as in a mirror (**c**), your child needs to focus on each letter at a time. For children starting to be confident reading in a language, it is a way to slow down the reading process and help your child focus on the details.

- Asking your child to write the text down will reinforce their attention to the details. Indeed, by just reading, your child can recognise a word overall without needing to have a close look at the details.

<u>**Variations**</u>:

Support:

- You can also provide a mirror to ease copying. Copying a text by looking in a mirror is still a challenge compared to reading directly a text (**c**).

Challenge!

- Ask your child to imagine, draw and write what follows (and/or precedes) the frame of the comic strip.

#49 The Letter Hunt

Preparation time: 🕒	**Minimum level of mastery of the language required** ☆☆/ 🕮🕮
Minimum number of participants: 1	**Material required**: Pen Paper

Aim of the activity: This activity is mainly designed for languages that have deep orthography [68] (i.e. a language that does not have one-to-one correspondence between sounds (phonemes[69]) and letters (graphemes[70]) that represent them).

- The aim is to spot the silent letters in a sentence.
- Alternatively, you can focus on one phoneme and the various corresponding graphemes.

Preparation of the resources:

- **Letter hunt**: Write one or two sentences that contain silent letters or various ways to spell one sound – graphemes – depending on the version you want to play.
- **Secret message**: Write a message with missing letters. All the letters missing correspond to the letters found in the "Letter hunt".

Instructions for the activity:

- Give your child the sentence(s) to "hunt" the letters. In the example below, your child would "hunt" for the sound [ε]:

Example:

Letter hunt:

Yesterday, I was sat on my beautiful red chair and I read a book with a very heavy hairy bear.

→ Letters found: 6 x E, 5x A, 2x I

---

[68] See glossary at the back for an explanation (p222-226).
[69] See glossary at the back for an explanation (p222-226).
[70] See glossary at the back for an explanation (p222-226).

Secret message: Your child needs to place all the letters found in the sentence above (i.e. 5 x E, 5x A, 2x I) in the sentence below:

W_ _r_ go_ng to h_v_ som_ c_r_mel _c_ - cr_ _m!!

→ The secret message was in this case: We are going to have some caramel ice-cream!!

Learning process and why it works:

- By "hunting"/looking for one specific sound, your child reinforces their knowledge of the different possible ways to spell it. Similarly, when looking for silent letters, the focus is put on the particular letters that are not heard, and can help your child notice them, and remember them more.
- The secret message serves two purposes:
  - It helps your child to see how the sound of letters can change according to the letters around.
  - As the number of missing letters correspond to the number of letters that should be found, your child can see immediately, if they did not spot some of them in the sentence(s) in the "Letter hunt".

Variations:

Support:

- Keep in mind that a message with missing letters is easier to read when the vowels are missing rather than the consonants.
- Have enough words without any missing letter in the secret message so that your child can guess the words that have missing letters more easily, and therefore only needs to place the appropriate letter in the gap.

  → Your child will therefore be able to work out the missing letters and then go back the "letter hunt" to find all the letters required.

Challenge!

- Ask your child to hunt more than one phoneme.

#50 The Fortune Teller

Preparation time:	Minimum level of mastery of the language required
⏲	☆☆/ 📖📖
Minimum number of participants: 2	**Material required**: Pen Paper
Aim of the activity: Writing short sentences.	

Preparation of the resources:

- Show your child how to fold a fortune teller out of a square piece of paper as below.

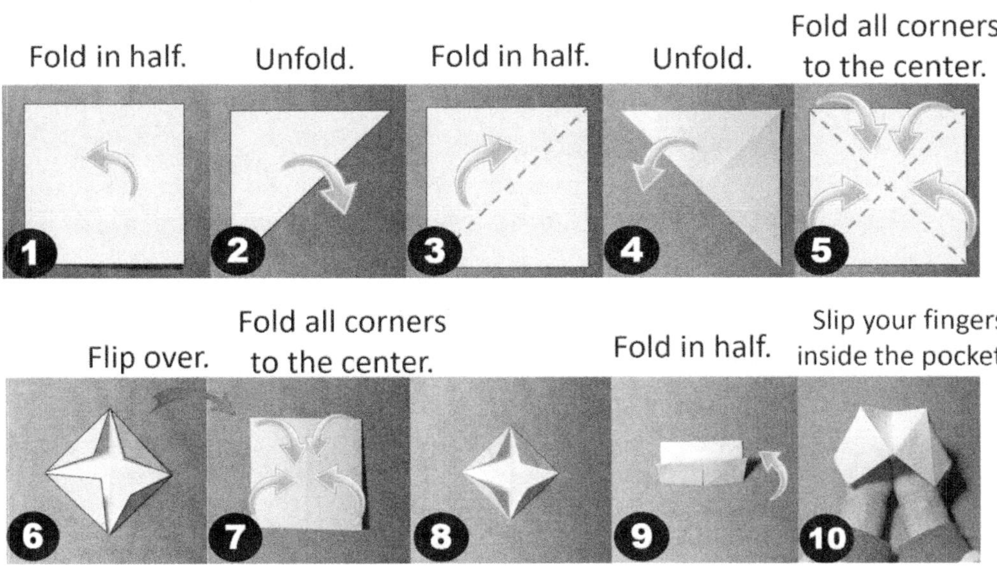

- Inside, ask your child to write the names of animals/colours/numbers. (See step ⑧ on the next page)
- Your child writes under each flap a statement. . (See step ⑨ on the next page). They could be a mix of nice and not-so-nice statements.
  They could, for example, take the form of "You are + adjective". Alternatively, they could be dares.

- With your child, write a list of words to spell out (e.g.: colours, animals, etc.)

At step 8 write names of animals on the flaps.

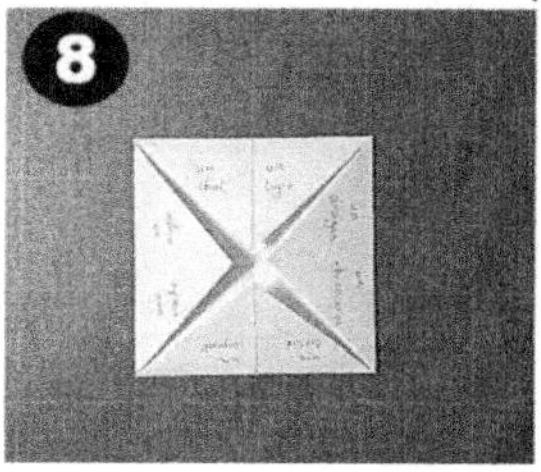

Open the flaps for your child to write comments.

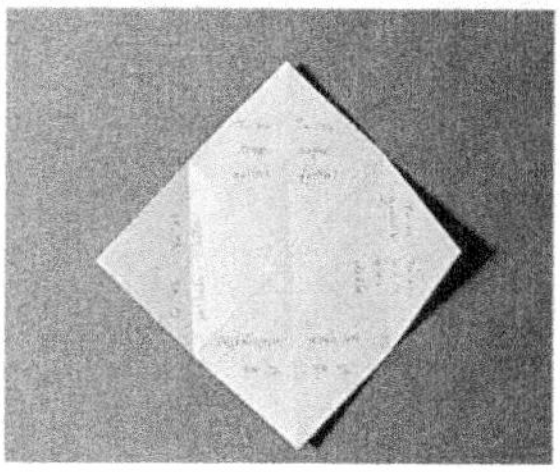

Fortune teller: ready to play

Instructions for the activity:

- Your child asks you to choose a word from the list you prepared together.
- They then spell it out. For each letter, they open the fortune teller in a different direction.
- Once the word is spelled out, they ask you to choose one of the four available options.
- You can then discover the statement/dare!

Learning process and why it works:

- Your child can write what they want (nice or silly!) This will motivate them to write.

Variations:

Support:

- Provide a structure, where only a few words need to be changed and write a model sentence down. Your child will therefore copy eight times the same words and replace those needed. E.g.: You are a + adjective ; You must + verb ; You have to say (*insert word*) ten times quickly ; Sing (*name of a song*).

#51 Calligram

Preparation time:	Minimum level of mastery of the language required
Minimum number of participants: 1	**Material required**: Pen Pencil Paper
Aim of the activity: Writing sentences for description purposes.	

Preparation of the resources:

- Here are two examples of calligram:

- For more examples, look online by searching "Guillaume Apollinaire calligram". He was a French poet known for the calligrams[71] he wrote.

Instructions for the activity:

- With a pencil, let your child draw what they want to write about.
- Let your child write about it by following the outline, or by filling the inside.

---

[71] Apollinaire, G., (2020) *Calligrammes : Poésie Visuelle*. Ed. Le Quichotte Littéraire

Learning process and why it works:

- The artistic aspect of the activity will help your child focus on details of the spelling, as they will want this artwork to be perfect!
- This should encourage your child to ask you about how to spell different words. Take this opportunity to return the question back to them, and let your child apply the knowledge they already have.
  E.g.: child - "How do you spell 'a feast'?"
  You – "It is the same [i:] sound as in 'heat'. How do you write 'heat'?"
  You can take this opportunity to guide your child with questions regarding other aspects, such as verb agreements[72].

Variations:

Support:

- Instead of several sentences, you can ask your child to repeat the same short sentence (or word) over and over. This will visually have the same effect, but it will be a copying exercise. By writing several times the same sentence or word, they will be able to work on their spelling.

Challenge!

- Write a poem by finding rhyming words.

---

[72] See glossary at the back for an explanation (p222-226).

#52 Le Cadavre Exquis

Preparation time: ⏲	Minimum level of mastery of the language required ☆☆/ 📖📖
Minimum number of participants: 3	**Material required**: Pen Paper
Aim of the activity: Sentence structure / syntax.	

"Le Cadavre exquis" is a game that was invented around 1925 by surrealist artists (mainly Jacques Prévert and Yves Tanguy).

Preparation of the resources:

- Decide on a sentence structure, and write an example.
- Include as many sections as there are players.
  E.g.: 3 players – Who / did what / where → Grandma / danced / in the garden.
  4 players – Opinion + "when" / who / does what / where → I like when / Grandma / dances / in the garden.

Note: If in the language you are teaching the verb agrees[73] with the subject, mention beforehand if the subject needs to be the 3rd person singular or plural.

Instructions for the activity:

- To each player assign one section to write.
- The first player writes their section at the top of the sheet, and then folds the paper backwards so that the section written is placed at the back of the sheet.
- The next player writes their section at the top of the sheet, and folds the paper in a similar way, and so on until all the players have written their part.

---

[73] See glossary at the back for an explanation (p222-226).

- None of the players should see or know what the previous ones wrote.
- You unfold the sheet and read the whole sentence, which is grammatically correct but would often be surprising or funny.

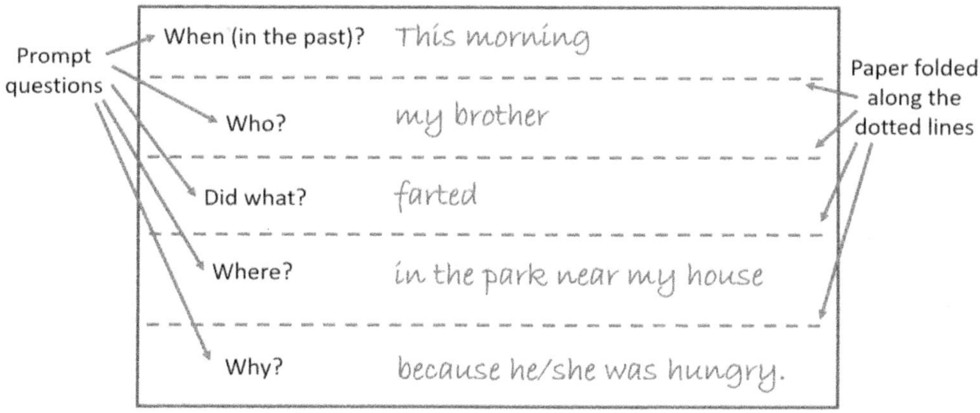

<u>**Learning process and why it works:**</u>

- Your child follows a certain order to write in. When children speak languages where the order of words is different, it can help consolidate their correct order.

- In languages that have particles indicating the grammatical function of a group of words, this exercise reinforces their knowledge and appropriate use.
  - In English, for example, " 's " indicates personal possession. E.g.: "Mark**'s** toy". When the word is plural and ends with an "s", only the apostrophe is required. E.g.: "My cousins**'** toy".
  - In Korean, **은/는** is placed after the subject of the sentence. If the subject ends with a consonant, 은 is used. And after a vowel, 는 is used.

<u>**Variations**</u>:

Support:

- Keep a dictionary at hand to help your child spell the words.

#53 Reinvent the Rules!

Preparation time: ◷◷	Minimum level of mastery of the language required ☆☆☆/ 🕮🕮
Minimum number of participants: 2	**Material required**: Pen Card paper Board game Dice Counters Printable board game available in the RESOURCES PACK on www.library4multilinguals.com
Aim of the activity: Writing short sentences. Transferring knowledge about spelling to write more creatively.	

Preparation of the resources:

- Use a board game you already have, create one, or use the one available in the RESOURCES PACK.
- When landing on some of the squares of the game, the players would need to draw a card with instructions.
- Create the instruction cards with your child (on card paper). There should be some with positive consequences, and others with negative ones. E.g.: Go back to the start; Join the player most advanced in the game; Skip your next turn; etc.

Note: This activity helps to show your child to use their knowledge learnt so far. If your child wants to write complex instructions that include words that are difficult to spell, help them to simplify or use alternatives with words they can already spell. Then, as much as possible, guide your child by referring to words they can already spell. E.g.: "'Dice' is spelled 'd' and 'ice' as in 'ice-cream'".

Instructions for the activity:

- Play the board game as normal, and draw a card every time you land on certain squares (primarily determined), or whenever the dice shows a certain number.

Learning process and why it works:

- Your child has complete freedom regarding the new rules they want to include in a game. This will be motivating enough to write sentences.
- Feeling like they can write anything that pleases them will help develop their confidence regarding writing.

Variations:

Support:

- Provide some example sentences for your child to copy and tweak.

III) Reading and writing short texts

Congratulations! Your child can now read a few sentences without being too intimidated, and they are showing curiosity and independence by trying to read various materials in the home language. This is all very positive! The hardest part is done, but your work is not over! You need to cultivate and nurture your child's interest and skills to help them access a higher level of literacy that will enable them to be truly independent.

Here are a few habits you should carry on in this respect:

Reading daily WITH/TO your child.

Having a routine where you read daily <u>to</u> your child is an important contributing factor to nurture your child's love of reading. Please note that the language in which you read the story does not really matter. What matters is to embed a pleasurable routine for your child that involves reading.

Even better would be to read <u>with</u> your child. This consists in you reading part of the story, and your child reading the rest. The more confident your child is, the more they can read. Gauge how much your child can and wants to read. You want this moment to stay a bonding moment, a pleasurable routine that your child looks forward to. You do not want your child starting to dread it because they feel like you are going to force them to read. Any kind of reading habit is good! You want to support your child in developing a love for reading in general.

Reading is not just about sounding out words. By reading with your child, you will be able to teach new words in context, and access books that are above their reading level, but that are easy enough to understand. See *Bonus activities to develop reading skills* at the back of the book (p215-217).

Create opportunities for PURPOSEFUL reading and writing.

Once our children can read, it can be tempting to just buy a workbook and follow it along, or to enrol your child in a Saturday school, and letting the school take full responsibility for teaching your child to read and write. However, it is very important that you also spend time "working" on their literacy while playing (which is the whole aim of this book).

When a child learns to read and write in the majority language, the skills learnt can easily be used outside the classroom. They are also used <u>purposefully</u>. When teaching the home language, we need to create opportunities for purposeful reading and writing. Here are a few ideas:

- Cooking/baking following a recipe book (in the home language).
- Leaving little notes written in your home language in your child's packed lunch.
- Writing a letter/email/messages to a family member or friend who does not understand the majority language of the country you live in.
- Starting a journal. (At the back of the book, you will also find *Tips to start journaling in a fun way* – p218-219).

Ultimately, you want your child to read independently. At this stage, most books would be too difficult to access alone. However, a fantastic book format to encourage your child to read independently are books written in the style of "100 questions about ...".

- The information is generally bite-size. Your child therefore does not need to read too much to get the whole information.
- Your child can just dip in and out, and start wherever they want. This makes it more likely to be reached out to as your child does not need to commit to putting prolonged effort. They can leave the book aside for a

couple of days or weeks before coming back to it without needing to remember what they read earlier to get the full benefit of it.

Let's discover some more activities that will help your child practise reading and writing in the home language while having fun!

#54 Start Over!

Preparation time:	Minimum level of mastery of the language required
Minimum number of participants: 2	**Material required**: Pen Paper
Aim of the activity: Reading longer texts. Focusing on the pronunciation of the words read.	

Preparation of the resources:

- Write five open questions with three answers to choose from for each one. One answer should be illogical. E.g.: *Where do you live? – I live with my parents, two brothers and a cat. - What is your favourite food? – I never ate fish.*
  (Look at the example on the next page)

- Choose one answer per question. Make a note of the answers you chose, on a piece of paper.

Instructions for the activity:

- You ask the questions to your child who needs to read one of the possible answers.
  - If the answer is the one you selected, you ask the next question.

- If the answer is not the one you chose, you read again the questions you previously asked from the first one.

- The aim of the game is to find all five correct answers in ten attempts maximum.

What is my magic spell word?
a) Abracadabra
b) Crunchy lettuce
c) Hocus pocus

What colour is my magic potion?
a) Green
b) Pink
c) Twelve

How many times do I need to repeat the spell word?
a) Silver
b) Three
c) Five

What is the secret ingredient of my magic potion?
a) Spider legs
b) Tasty
c) Dinosaur eggshell

What does my magic potion do?
a) It gives you incredible strength
b) You become invisible
c) Freeze it in your freezer

Note 1: As one of the three answers to choose from for each question does not answer it, it should not be chosen by your child. Therefore your child only needs to choose between two answers each time. By carefully reading the possible answers, even if your child ends up choosing the wrong option each time, they can find all the combinations in ten attempts maximum. By paying attention your child has 100% chances to win the game.

Note 2: To encourage your child to read accurately, count any word misread or invented answer, as a failed attempt, and start over.

Note 3: Feel free to make the answers as short or long as you wish to suit your child's level.

<u>Learning process and why it works:</u>

- Your child will need to read carefully the options to work out the one that does not answer the question. This is a way to encourage your child to, not only decipher the words, but to understand what they are reading.

<u>Variations</u>:

Support

- Make the questions about a fictional character or a person that your child knows. They need to work out which character they are. Working out little by little who it is will guide your child to choose the right answers for the last questions, making sure your child can guess who is being described.

1) How many siblings do I have? a) one brother b) two sisters c) none	3) I am a ... a) girl b) boy c) cat	5) What is my name? a) Puss in Boots b) Cinderella c) Hansel
2) Where does the evil character live? a) a castle b) a big house c) a gingerbread house	4) What do I have on my feet? a) normal shoes b) boots c) glass slippers	

#55. 21 Dares

Preparation time: ⏲	**Minimum level of mastery of the language required** ☆/ 📖📖
Minimum number of participants: 2	**Material required**: Written text
Aim of the activity: The focus is on the pronunciation of the words read.	

Preparation of the resources:

- Choose a paragraph in your child's favourite book (or any other one)

Instructions for the activity:

- In turns, each player reads one, two, or three words (from the start to the end of the paragraph)
- The player who ends up reading the last word loses and needs to do a dare that the other player(s) decides.

Notes:

- For simplicity, consider that two words are separated by a space. i.e. "it is" = 2 words; "it's" = 1 word.
- Feel free to correct your child's pronunciation. The lack of impact of the mispronunciation or the difficulty to read makes it a safe place for your child to hear and accept your guidance and correction.
- For your child to consolidate their learning, you can play the game twice (or more) using the same text.

Example:

Text to read	How **Player A** and *Player B* could play:
Once upon a time, there was a boy who lived in a little cottage with his parents and four brothers. He was the youngest and the tiniest of the family.	**Once - upon** ; *a – time - there* ; **was** ; *a - boy - who* ; **lived - in - a** ; *little - cottage - with* ; **his - parents** ; *and - four* ; **brothers. - He - was** ; *the - youngest* ; **and** ; *the - tiniest - of* ; **the** ; *family*. (Player B lost as they said the last word)

Learning process and why it works:

- Your child will be thinking strategically about the number of words they will read out loud. The reading pace is therefore slow and gives enough time to correct mispronunciation if necessary.
- Your child only needs to read one, two, or three words at a time and is therefore more likely to carry on reading for a long time.

Variations:

Challenge!

- You can follow this activity by asking your child to find in the text, synonyms[74] or antonyms[75] of certain words. You can also give the definition of a word to be found. It is also possible to ask for translations by saying a word or expression in the majority language and asking your child to find the corresponding expression or word in the text.

[74] See glossary at the back for an explanation (p222-226).
[75] See glossary at the back for an explanation (p222-226).

#56 Guided Colouring

Preparation time: ⏲	Minimum level of mastery of the language required ☆☆/ 🕮🕮
Minimum number of participants: 1	**Material required**: colouring book (or any drawing that can be coloured) pen paper Templates available in the RESOURCES PACK on www.library4multilinguals.com
Aim of the activity: Understanding instructions	

Preparation of the resources:

- Find an image your child can colour, and print it out (or take one from a colouring book)
- Write a text explaining how to colour it. E.g.: The tortoise's legs are green.

Example:

The tortoise is dancing! Its head, legs and tail are green. But be careful, its nails are grey.
The front of the shell is yellow, and the back is brown.
The tortoise likes the music! The notes are pink, green, and blue [...]

Instructions for the activity:

- Give the instructions and the drawing to your child to colour.
- Then compare the drawing with the instructions.
- If you coloured one yourself as well, your child can compare their drawing with yours. For every difference, read with your child the instructions and see what was written.

You can make deliberate mistakes. Your child will be happy to see that they understood the text better than you!

Note: The first time you do this activity, you can print one for yourself to colour according to the description you have written. You can do it at the same time as your child and model out loud how you do it.

Learning process and why it works:

- This activity offers a good balance between the effort your child needs to put in to read and understand the instructions, and the peaceful colouring activity.

Variations:

Support:

- Write short sentences that have a very similar structure. E.g.: "Find the *(element in the picture)*. It is *(colour)*."

Challenge!

- Include distractions. For example, mention that usually one element should be one colour, but in this drawing, it is different.
  E.g.: It is well known that dogs are generally black, white, or brown. Well, this one is blue!
- For creative children, this activity can feel a little too constraining. In that case, write a text and leave some words out.
  E.g.: This beautiful dog is all ____________ with bright ____________ spots. Her eyes are ________________. Have you noticed that she has a ________________ shaped spot under her left eye?
  Note that this presents an ideal opportunity to work on adjective agreements[76] for languages where the adjective changes according to the noun it describes.

[76] See glossary at the back for an explanation (p222-226).

#57 Uncover the Message

Preparation time:	Minimum level of mastery of the language required
Minimum number of participants: 2	**Material required**: Text
Aim of the activity: Predicting the words that follow, and the meaning.	

Preparation of the resources:

- Select a paragraph of a book that matches your child's level of understanding.

Instructions for the activity:

- With your finger, a ruler, or a bookmark, hide the line your child is reading, and reveal the words little by little.
- Your child works out the words by seeing the first letters, from the context and their places in the sentence.

Note: From the different clues your child should even be able to work out the words before they see the first letter. In that case, it can be good to let your child give you several options before revealing the first letter(s). Whenever the word given is not logical due to what was mentioned before, you can refer back to it so that your child does not just start guessing randomly, but carries on working things out.

Learning process and why it works:

- In order to work out the words that follow, your child needs both, to keep in mind the meaning of the words and sentences previously read, and to use the visual clues (i.e. letters, capital vs lowercase, punctuation).
- This is also an excellent activity to consolidate the understanding of the syntax that is proper to the home language.

Variations:

Support:

- Use a text that your child has already read. This could be a bedtime story they are familiar with.

Challenge!

- Ask about how certain words are spelled (e.g.: spelling of verb endings) before you uncover them.

#57b The Covered Message

Preparation time:	Minimum level of mastery of the language required
🕐	☆☆/ 🕮🕮
Minimum number of participants: 1	**Material required**: Text Random objects to cover parts of the text
Aim of the activity: Predicting the hidden words according to the visible clues. Consolidation of sentence structure proper to the home language.	

Preparation of the resources:

- Select a paragraph of a book that matches your child's level of understanding.

Instructions for the activity:

- With little objects, cover the text.
- Make sure that enough parts of the words and sentences are visible for your child to be able to work out the hidden parts.

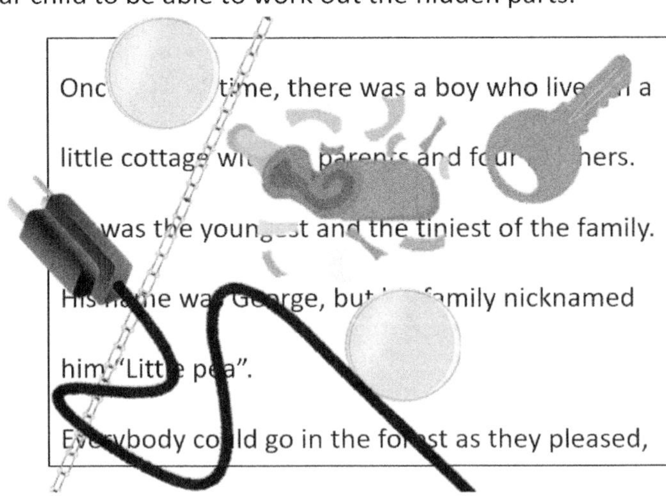

Learning process and why it works:

- In order to work out the words that follow, your child needs both, to keep in mind the meaning of the words and sentences previously read, and to use the visual clues (i.e. letters, capital vs lowercase, punctuation, spaces between visible words).
- This is also an excellent activity to consolidate the understanding of the syntax that is proper to the home language.

Variations:

Support:

- Use a text that your child has already read. This could be a bedtime story they are familiar with.

Challenge!

- Ask about how certain words are spelled (e.g.: spelling of verb endings) before you uncover them.

#58 Preparing an Outing

Preparation time:	Minimum level of mastery of the language required
⌚⌚	☆☆/ 📖📖
Minimum number of participants: 1	**Material required**: Pen Paper
Aim of the activity: Enriching the experience of an outing by providing questions and information before getting to the place you will be visiting.	

Preparation of the resources:

- Gather some fun facts about a place you are going to visit (e.g.: museum, forest) or an activity you have not done together before (e.g.: fishing).
- Write them in the form of a questionnaire, a true or false, or questions with multiple choice answers. These will help your child appreciate the outing fully and the question format avoids your child wondering why you had to write it and could not just tell them. It also helps them being more curious about the place or activity they are going to discover!

Here is an example with questions that will encourage your child to observe, wonder, and search for answers.

THE NATURAL HISTORY MUSEUM OF LONDON

What function did they serve?

____

____

____

____

____

On old buildings, you can see such statues called "Gargoyles".
Can you find some on the Natural History Museum?
What do they look like?
(Draw one below)

There is a skeleton of this animal displayed in the central hall.
What is the name of this animal?

____

How many ribs does it have? (Count them on the skeleton: ______

There is a statue of this very famous scientist. It is on the landing of the central hall. What is his name?

____

What is he famous for?

____

____

____

Instructions for the activity:

- Before starting the visit or the activity, give the questionnaire to your child to complete. This would ideally be done when they would need to wait without anything to do (e.g.: in the queue before entering the museum, or when you are preparing the fishing gear).
- The visit or activity should help your child get more out of the visit or help him put new knowledge into practice.

Learning process and why it works:

- Your child will be learning facts that are interesting, fun, surprising or even intriguing. The activity that follows demonstrates by itself the relevance of what they read. This will help your child engage in the reading activity.

Variations:

Support:

- By writing the questions yourself you can pitch the level exactly to their level. Use multiple choice or true or false types of questions so that your child is intrigued by the questions but does not spend too much time searching for the answers.

Challenge!

- You can use children's encyclopaedias, or other child friendly texts. Your child will need to find the answers to your questions in these texts/books.

#59 Close Inspection

Preparation time:	Minimum level of mastery of the language required
Minimum number of participants: 1	**Material required**: Word processor Printer Alternatively: pen and paper
Aim of the activity: This activity will help your child proofread their writing.	

Preparation of the resources:

- Write two nearly identical texts.
- Include mistakes in one or the other text. (There should be mistakes in both texts)
- Make sure you leave enough space between the lines for your child to write the corrections.

Note: To help with your child's engagement, make the text relevant by referring to things that happened recently to your child, and/or by incorporating names of his favourite characters.

Instructions for the activity:

- Your child needs to read the two texts and compare them.
- They will notice some differences in the spelling of some words, words missing, or words not placed in the right place.
- Each time your child needs to decide which option is the correct one – the one in text A or text B. (The differences between the two texts are circled in the example)

Text A

Yesterday, we went to the park. As the whether was nice, we had a piknik. I ate two sandwiches. My bely became big and round like a football. But I still had a chocolate ice cream! I can't say no to a delicous ice cream!

Text B

Yesterday, we went the park. As the weather was nice, we had a picnic. I ate two sandwichs. My belly became big and round like a football. But I still had a chocolate icecream! I cant say no to a delicious ice cream!

Learning process and why it works:

- Include mistakes that your child is generally making and help them decide which one is the correct option by reiterating rules they would know.
- The activity enables you to guide your child step-by-step and model the proofreading process by making mistakes obvious.

Variations:

Support:

- Focus on not more than a couple of types of mistakes (e.g.: noun-adjective word order, verb ending of a particular tense).

Challenge!

- Only have one text and mention the types of mistakes and how many there are. E.g.: 5 mistakes with present tense verbs, 3 mistakes with capital letters.

#60 That's Not True!

Preparation time: ⏲	Minimum level of mastery of the language required ☆☆/ 📖📖
Minimum number of participants: 1	**Material required**: Pen Paper
Aim of the activity: Reading and understanding short texts.	

Preparation of the resources:

- Write a short paragraph about something that is relevant to your child. It could be what they did during the day, a book you recently read together, etc. Include a few details that are inaccurate. E.g.: Your child ate toasts for breakfast, but the text mentions that they ate a banana.

Instructions for the activity:

- Your child reads the text and needs to find the inaccuracies and correct them.

Learning process and why it works:

- By making the text relevant to your child, they will want to know what it is about, and will be eager to find the inaccuracies.
- By being emotionally engaged, your child will pay closer attention to details.

Variations:

Support:

- Include names, numbers, and make sure that some of the mistakes incorporate them. This will help your child spot them easily.

Challenge!

- Include grammatical mistakes (word order, verb agreements[77], adjective agreements[78], spelling ...) for your child to spot them. If they do not notice them, mention them, and see if they can correct them. So that it does not look like you are testing your child's knowledge, mention them casually. E.g.: "Oh! Look how I wrote this! I wrote 'two'! So how should I have written 'bird'?"

---

[77] See glossary at the back for an explanation (p222-226).

[78] See glossary at the back for an explanation (p222-226).

#61 Spot the mistakes

Preparation time: ◷	**Minimum level of mastery of the language required** ☆☆/ 📖📖
Minimum number of participants: 1	**Material required**: Pen Paper Picture or illustrations
Aim of the activity: Paying attention to details in texts.	

Preparation of the resources:

- Find a photo or an illustration.
- Write a description of the picture with some differences.
- Indicate how many differences your child needs to spot.

Instructions for the activity:

- Your child reads the description and looks at the illustration.
- They need to spot the differences and correct them.

See example[79] below:

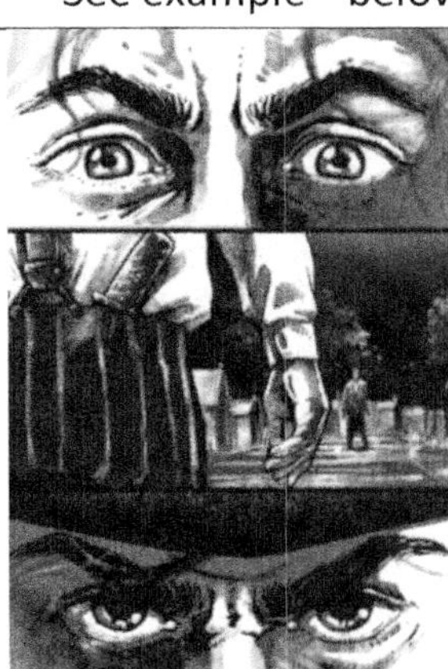	The scene takes place at night. We can see two men about to race each other. The man at the top looks surprised or frightened, and the one at the bottom seems happy. He is wearing a hat. I can see that the man is hiding a gun in his stripy trousers. He is wearing a black shirt.

[79] This illustration is taken from the novel *Enfermé* by Yoshito Darmon-Shimamori, a fantasy novel aimed at French speaking teenagers to improve their literacy and knowledge of the French culture while enjoying a good story! Estimated publication date: December 2021.

Learning process and why it works:

- This exercise helps your child read the written text in detail.
- Giving a visual support guides your child when processing the information written as most of what is written can be seen as well.

Variations:

Support:

- Specify the types of differences there could be. E.g.: colours, number of people/animal/object present, action, etc.

Challenge!

- In your description, mention what could happen, or what must have happened before. Your child will have to interpret what is happening in the picture.

#62 Spot the Non-Sense

Preparation time: ⏲	**Minimum level of mastery of the language required** ☆☆/ 📖📖
Minimum number of participants: 1	**Material required**: Pen Paper
Aim of the activity: This activity will help your child pay attention and reflect on the choice of words.	

Preparation of the resources:

- Write a short text and include parts that do not make logical sense.
  E.g.: *"He was so tired that he decided to run around."* (the tiredness does not match the decision) *"She put her shoes on but went outside."* (the conjunction "*but*" is not appropriate).

Note: Write a text that is relevant to your child. Refer to what has happened recently and people in their life so that they can also identify and understand emotionally the different people mentioned, and have a better understanding of the situation depicted. This will help them identify the parts that do not make sense.

Instructions for the activity:

- Your child reads the text and needs to identify the parts of the text that do not make logical sense.
- They then need to replace them with something that is logical. Of course, there is often more than one possible answer.

Learning process and why it works:

- It is often easier to spot mistakes in a text we have not written ourselves.

- By correcting a work they have not produced, and where they know there are parts that do not make sense, your child will be able to identify what needs to be done to write a good quality text.
- This activity will help your child improve the quality of the texts they write.

Variations:

Support:

- Finding the "non-sense" needs good agility of the language. To start with, and to make the task less daunting, include "lies" instead of "non-sense".

  E.g.1: if your child has a cute little brother, you could write *"my cute big brother"*.

  E.g.2: At dinner, if your child who hates mushrooms said *"I don't want to eat the mushrooms. They are disgusting"*, you could report this event and write that your child said *"I want to eat more mushrooms. They are delicious!"*

  This exercise will be more emotionally charged, and your child will have fun correcting the text to establish the truth!

  Within this text, you could slip a couple of "non-sense". Your child might notice them. In that case, congratulate them and work out together what would make more sense. (If your child does not notice them, do it, and then work out what would be more appropriate).

  The following times, you will be able to include more nonsense parts in the text.

Challenge!

- Omit words or parts of sentences. Your child will need to work out, from what is before and after, what word(s) are missing, and write them.

#63 Swap

Preparation time:	Minimum level of mastery of the language required
Minimum number of participants: 1	**Material required**: Word processor Printer
Aim of the activity: Helping the child notice the words being used to improve their own use of words when speaking or writing. **Consider this activity is a step up from "#62 Spot the non-sense" activity.**	

Preparation of the resources:

- Write a text about what your child has done recently for example (or anything else that would be relevant to your child)
- Swap words in the text two by two (either from different grammatical categories, or from similar ones), and highlight them.
  E.g.: *Yesterday, daddy read you a* ***fell*** *before* ***think****. However, he* ***story*** *asleep before you! Next time, maybe you need to choose a shorter book. Don't you* ***bed****?*

Instructions for the activity:

- Your child reads the text and needs to work out which words have been swapped.
- They will look at the other highlighted words in the text that could fit.
- They rewrite the words in their right places.

Note: Make sure you do not swap too many words. The text should still be understandable.

Learning process and why it works:

- By reading a text, a child (or any language learner) will accept the text as being correct and will only focus on understanding the overall message. It does not mean that they will be able to transfer choice of words or their order when speaking or writing.
  By swapping words, your child will pay closer attention to the meaning of the sentences. They will guestimate the word that should be in the sentence instead of the highlighted one. The other highlighted words offer a limited number of options to choose from.

Variations:

Support:

- Swap words that are from different grammatical categories. While reading, your child will understand immediately that the sentence does not make sense, and will be able to guess the word that should be written in its place more easily. They will therefore only need to find that word or a synonym[80].

Challenge!

- Do not highlight the swapped words. And mention how many words have been swapped.
- Swap homophones[81]: This will help your child focus on spelling.
- Swap words that are of the same grammatical category (e.g. verbs, adjectives, nouns, ...) so that the sentence is grammatically correct. Your child will have to look closer at the meaning of what they are reading.

[80] See glossary at the back for an explanation (p222-226).
[81] See glossary at the back for an explanation (p222-226).

#64 The Storyteller

Preparation time:	Minimum level of mastery of the language required
⏲	☆☆/ 📖📖📖
Minimum number of participants: 1	**Material required**: Book Sound recording device (on most mobile phones) Soundtrack (many soundtracks can be downloaded for free for personal use) Example video available on www.library4multilinguals.com
Aim of the activity: Reading accuracy. (Only do this activity when your child is starting to read fluently. If they are still at a deciphering stage, it will generate frustration).	

Preparation of the resources:

- Ask your child to choose a book they want to read out loud.
- Find a music/soundtrack that goes with the mood of the extract your child is going to read.

Instructions for the activity:

- Start playing the soundtrack. Your child starts reading the extract. You record everything.
- You play it back to listen to it with the book in front of your child (and you). They will naturally spot any mistakes made and will want to record it again to get it right.

Learning process and why it works:

- The soundtrack will help your child feel like it is similar to the storytellers they might have seen on TV or to the audio books they have listened to. They will therefore want the recording to be perfect!

- For children who are at a stage where they read too fast (i.e. they make quite a few mistakes without realising it) this activity helps them notice their own mistakes when checking the recording and reading the text at the same time. Over time, it will lead to greater accuracy.

<u>Variations</u>:

Support:

- With your child, choose a book that they are already familiar with.

#65 Running Dictation

Preparation time: ◷	Minimum level of mastery of the language required ☆/ 🕮🕮
Minimum number of participants: 1	**Material required**: Pen Paper Extract of a book Optional: Timer
Aim of the activity: Spelling accuracy.	

Preparation of the resources:

- At a desk, set a pen and paper.
- Choose a paragraph in a book (or write your own text) and leave it in a place far away from the desk.

Instructions for the activity:

- Your child needs to go to the text you wrote and then go back to the desk to write it down.
- They are not allowed to touch the text. They can only read it.
- Insist on the fact that everything needs to be completely accurate: spelling, capital letters, and punctuation.

- They can remember a small part of it, and then go back to the desk to write the message down. This needs to be repeated until the whole text is copied.
- Depending on the length of the text copied and your child's proficiency, you can then either tell your child the number of mistakes there are in their text, or underline the words that contain mistakes.
- You can then decide to carry on the game with your child having to run to the text again to check the mistakes, or bring the text to the desk so that your child can compare both versions and spot their own mistakes. This could be an opportunity to go over certain grammar, conjugation, or spelling points (depending on your child's knowledge).

Note: If more than one child is doing the activity, partner A can run to the text and come back to tell partner B the words they can remember. Partner B writes. (Make sure, partner A does not just read out loud the text for partner B to write). They can then swap roles. You can also organise this as a competition between the children who need to copy their own texts.

<u>**Learning process and why it works:**</u>

- Due to the distance between the text to copy and the desk, your child must keep in their memory the words to write and their spelling for a longer time than if they were only copying. This effort will help the memorisation of spelling.

- The necessity to copy everything accurately and having to correct the mistakes helps your child pay attention to them.

<u>Variations</u>:

Support:

- Write five short sentences and number them. When pointing at the mistakes, you can either mention the number of the sentence or underline the words containing them.
- Base your text on a certain point you are helping your child to master (e.g.: certain verb tenses, graphemes, word order, *kanji*[82], etc.)

Challenge!

- Once your child has copied the text, underline the words that contain mistakes for your child to work out the mistakes (without checking the text they copied). If needed, guide your child by asking the questions they ought to ask themself to work them out.

[82] See glossary at the back for an explanation (p222-226).

#66 Spot the Homophone[83]

Preparation time:	Minimum level of mastery of the language required
Minimum number of participants: 1	**Material required:** Pen Paper
Aim of the activity: Spelling	

Note: To play this game, your child should already be aware of what homophones are. Be aware that introducing this game too early could confuse your child. They need to know securely at least a few homophones. This activity is perfect to deepen their knowledge. It should not be used to introduce the concept of "homophone".

Preparation of the resources:

- Write a text by spelling some words as their homophones.
  E.g.: I have never ***bean*** so happy ***end*** sad at the same ***thyme***.

Instructions for the activity:

- Your child needs to spot all the homophones and write them with their correct spelling.
- Make sure to ask your child what the homophones mean or to put them in a sentence. If your child does not know the homophone, explain it.

Learning process and why it works:

- As your child knows that they need to find the homophones, they will therefore pay more attention to them. By spotting them it will make them more aware of their differences.

Variations:

Support:

- Mention how many homophones your child needs to spot.

[83] See glossary at the back for an explanation (p222-226).

#67 Child Teacher

Preparation time:	Minimum level of mastery of the language required
◷	☆☆/ 📖📖
Minimum number of participants: 2	**Material required**: Pen Paper Text for dictation
Aim of the activity: Spelling accuracy / proofreading	

Preparation of the resources:

- Ask your child to choose a text that they will dictate to you.
- Provide your child with options. Ensure that the texts are of the appropriate level at which your child can write.

Instructions for the activity:

- Your child dictates the text for you to write. Make sure they mention the punctuation as well.
- Write it mostly accurately. Include the type of mistakes your child makes. You can focus on a few types of mistakes.
- Then your child compares your text with the one they read and circles the mistakes.
- Ask your child why the way you wrote it was wrong. If your child cannot explain, guide your child with questions and alternatives. This exercise models proofreading.
  - E.g.1: You write "*I **red** this book*". Your child could explain "'red' is the colour, but when you read a book, you write it '*read*'"
  - E.g.2: You write "*On **Wensday**, I went to the beach*". Your child could explain "It sounds like 'Wensday', but you have to spell it 'Wednesday'".

Notes:

- Avoid justifications such as "*That's just the way it is*". For words with "tricky" spelling, find mnemonics[84] to help your child remember, explain where the spelling is coming from, or pronounce it the way it is spelled. This exercise should give keys to your child to help them write accurately.
- If a word has been borrowed from another language your child knows, or is a cognate[85], use them to make it memorable, and show in the meantime the advantage of being able to read and write in more than one language.

Learning process and why it works:

- It can be a negative experience to make mistakes. Correcting someone else's mistakes is emotionally much more bearable. Therefore, your child can learn a lot better from this exercise than by doing a traditional dictation where the adult corrects their mistakes.

Variations:

Support:

- Include mistakes that can be spotted easily, such as punctuation.
- At the beginning, ask for a dictation that is no more than five sentences long in order to focus only on a small number of mistakes.

Challenge!

- Let your child choose a text in any of the books they are reading.

[84] See glossary at the back for an explanation (p222-226).
[85] See glossary at the back for an explanation (p222-226).

#68 Complete the Speech Bubbles

Preparation time: 🕐	**Minimum level of mastery of the language required** ☆☆/ 📖📖
Minimum number of participants: 1	**Material required**: Pen Paper Comic strip Printer Camera Templates available as part of the RESOURCES PACK on www.library4multilinguals.com
Aim of the activity: Creative writing	

Preparation of the resources:

- Take a picture of a comic strip.
- Erase the text on a photo editing software, and print it out. Alternatively, print out the comic strip and cut out the speech bubbles. Then stick it over a sheet of paper.
- You can also find children's book without a single word written such as David Wiesner's beautiful *Sector 7*.

Instructions for the activity:

- Your child looks at the images and imagines what the characters could be saying, and completes the speech bubbles accordingly.

Learning process and why it works:

- This activity provides a good balance between freedom and guidance, and your child will be inspired to write a short story.
- The story does not need to be similar to the one intended by the author. The story could be completely different. The aim is simply to match logically the content of the speech bubbles with the action depicted in each frame of the comic strip.

Variations:

Support:

- Discuss with your child what is happening in the picture to help them spot all the relevant details. Help your child simplify what they want to write to use words that they can spell. This task is challenging, but by choosing words that are simpler to spell, your child will feel a sense of achievement.
- You could also provide a couple of lines that your child needs to copy in the right speech bubble to get them going.

Challenge!

- Take a picture of a whole comic strip (or take the main frames), remove the text, and separate all the pictures. Your child needs to put the pictures in order and write the text. Note that the pictures do not need to be in the same order as in the original version. However the texts written in the speech bubbles need to match logically.

#69 A Pen and a Dice

Preparation time:	Minimum level of mastery of the language required
🕐	☆☆/ 📖📖
Minimum number of participants: 1	**Material required**: Pen Paper Dice Stopwatch
Aim of the activity: Consolidating the knowledge of the sentence structure in the home language + Manipulation of different aspects of the home language such as registers[86] and verb tenses.	

Due to having less exposure and use of the home language, compared to the school/community language, a bilingual / multilingual child commonly faces the following difficulties:

a) They can map the sentence structure of the strongest onto the weaker one. E.g.: In spoken English, you can finish a sentence with a preposition and ask "*Who did you go **with**?*" Transposed into French, it could become "*Qui tu es allé(e) **avec**?*" instead of "***Avec** qui tu es allé(e)?*"

b) They might not be comfortable using different registers in their home language(s) as they are in the majority one.

This activity aims to increase your child's awareness and knowledge of the above.

Preparation of the resources:

- Write down two sets of five sentences (i.e. ten in total) in one language to be translated or changed into another register or tense for example.

Instructions for the activity:

[86] See glossary at the back for an explanation (p222-226).

- Explain to your child that they are going to translate/change five sentences and see how long it takes them. However, they can only write if they throw a 6 with the dice. You cannot give any answer but can guide them exclusively by asking questions. This helps model the thinking process. You time everything. Your child then has a second round to check if they improve.
- Provide the sheet with the first five sentences to your child who can read them. Then start the stopwatch.
- Your child throws the dice to get a 6. Only then can they translate/change the first sentence.
- Once the first sentence is written, they throw the dice again to try and get a 6 to be able to write the second sentence.
- The process is repeated until they have written down the five sentences.
- See on the stopwatch how long it took them to complete the task.
- At the end, "debrief" with your child! What were the stumble blocks? What did they learn?
- Repeat the process with the next five sentences you prepared.
- At the end, compare the time it took to your child to complete the task, and reflect on what they remembered the second time.

Learning process and why it works:

- The second round will ensure that your child pays attention to all the feedback you give so that they can improve in the second round. Please note that it is important to mention that there will be a second round to remove the pressure from getting everything right in the first go.
- The dice ensures that there is a part left to chance and that not everything is based on knowledge.

Variations:

Support:

- Only focus on one point E.g.: word order, verb agreements[87], adjective agreements[88], specific graphemes[89], homophones[90], etc.

Challenge!

- Include a variety of points to focus on.

---

[87] See glossary at the back for an explanation (p222-226).
[88] See glossary at the back for an explanation (p222-226).
[89] See glossary at the back for an explanation (p222-226).
[90] See glossary at the back for an explanation (p222-226).

#70 Ping-Pong Writing

Preparation time:	**Minimum level of mastery of the language required**
Minimum number of participants: 2	**Material required**: Pen Paper Box/hat/envelope
Aim of the activity: Creative writing	

Preparation of the resources:

- With your child, decide on the genre of the story you want to write together.
- With your child, write words and expressions that you will need to include in your story. Write one word or expression per piece of paper.
- Fold them and place them in a box, a hat, or an envelope.

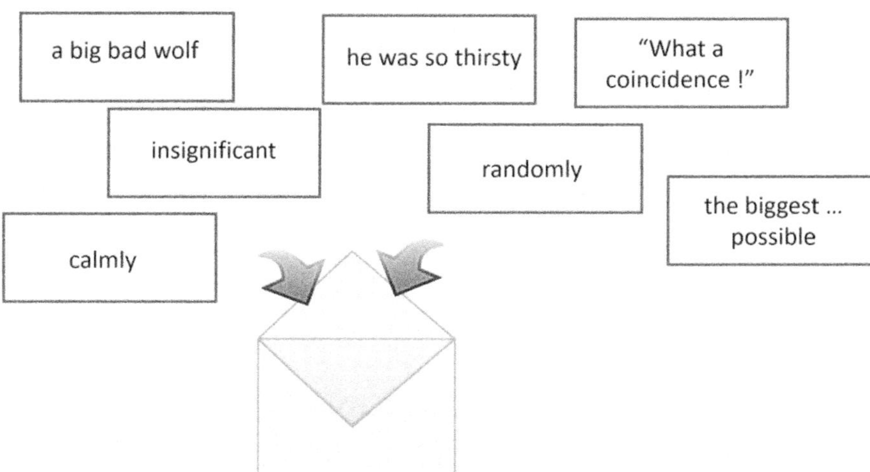

Instructions for the activity:

- Pick a paper randomly from the box containing all the words you have written. Then start writing the story until you use the word on the paper. Therefore, the sentence does not need to be finished.

- Your child then picks a paper and carries on the story until they can include the expression/word.
- Take turns and repeat the process until the story is finished.
- If you use all the words before the story ends, put them back in the envelope and pick a word again.

Learning process and why it works:

- The aim of this activity is to get your child to write creatively in a fun way.
- Writing a story with your help will appear much more achievable than on their own.
- The words on the papers that can appear as constraints will provide you and your child ideas to carry on with the story.

Variations:

Support:

- Try to retell a short story or a tale that your child chooses. It will give you guidelines, but the story will inevitably be twisted due to the words you pick out of the envelope.

Let's take the example of *Jack and the Beanstalk* and add the words in the example on the previous page. **Writer 1 is represented by the bold writing**, *writer 2 by italics*, and the expressions from the envelope are underlined.

> **Once upon a time, there was a boy called Jack, who lived with a big bad wolf** *in a little cottage. The big bad wolf ate everything. One day, there was nothing left for Jack to eat. He was so thirsty and hungry!* ***So he decided to go to market to sell their cow. When he arrived, he met a girl who was very hungry and wanted to sell her cow too! "What a coincidence!" they exclaimed.*** [...]

Challenge!

- You can use the story outline template to guide you when writing the story, and let your child's imagination and yours go wild.

Most stories follow the structure below:

- **An opener** where you present who the story is about and establish a problem, a challenge they face.
- **An event that challenges everything** and incites the main character to go on a journey.
- **Obstacles** that the main character needs to overcome.
- **The climax** where the main character seems to have failed on their journey.
- **The end** where all the problems are resolved.

#71 The Incomplete Manuscript

Preparation time: 🕑🕑	**Minimum level of mastery of the language required** ☆☆☆/ 🕮🕮🕮
Minimum number of participants: 1	**Material required**: Pen Paper
Aim of the activity: Creative writing	

Preparation of the resources:

- Write an incomplete short story. Leave some blank spaces after words that suggest additional key information, or a twist in the story such as "suddenly, meanwhile, he heard a little noise coming from …"

  Optional: Feel free to tear up the paper to make it look like you found an old lost manuscript. You can also make it look stained with ink or coffee. Illustrations can also serve as great prompts.

Instructions for the activity:

- Announce to your child that you found a lost manuscript.
- Ask your child to read the different visible parts.
- Then discuss what could be the missing parts of the story.
- Let your child take the lead on the ideas and assist them with the writing part of the task (if necessary).

Note: The more care you will put in the *mise-en-scène* of the activity, the more your child will be inspired to write the missing parts.

Learning process and why it works:

- Children have a lot of imagination. It is however difficult to organise all these ideas into a coherent and interesting story. The little parts of the story that you provide will help your child to creatively fill in the gaps.

Variations:

Support:

- Only leaving small gaps in the story that require descriptions. The overall storyline will be clear, and your child will need to provide all the details that will make the story come to life!

Challenge!

- Provide a minimum number of elements to start with. It could be the moral of the story, the nickname of a character and some personality traits, a few unfinished and dramatic sentences (e.g.: we heard a big BANG! It was coming from...)

Bonus activities to develop reading skills

Reading a book can be done in various ways to suit different purposes. Of course, the main objective is to help our children enjoy the stories they discover in them. To get to the stage where they can do it independently, we need to model, and guide them.

It is common for multilingual children to feel like they cannot access a book in their weaker language(s) due to lack of vocabulary, or difficulty in deciphering words if the script is different. If they are not as fluent reading in their weaker language(s), they can naturally feel less inclined to pick up a book in that language. Consequently, they will have less exposure and practice, and the gap between their languages becomes wider. It is a vicious circle.

Here are a few activities that can be done to support your child's literacy skills in general, and in their home language(s).

Reading TO your child:

This is the most obvious way of reading that we have all done with our children. However, it has to be stressed that this activity should not stop when your child starts to be able to read. There are indeed many benefits to it, and should be carried on as long as possible.

By reading TO your child, you can choose books that are slightly above your child's level. As a more proficient reader, you are able to read, decipher complex words, and pause appropriately. This can help your child work out from the context many new words. You can as well clarify anything whenever necessary and help your child fully appreciate the story. This practice will also make you more aware of your child's precise reading level and will be able to find new appropriate books more easily.

Multilingual children generally have stronger reading skills in their school language. By reading to your child, you are therefore enabling them to access books with stories that are suitable for their age range. Consequently, you are exposing them to more complex words and expressions, which will help them widen their vocabulary.

As this activity represents less effort, a child generally feels more inclined to ask questions and understand a story in detail. It is therefore an adequate moment to work on inference (See p218).

Reading WITH your child:

This activity can be seen as a step up from the previous one, as your child who can now read, starts reading parts of the story. You can share them equally by reading a paragraph or a page each. But while your child is still at a deciphering stage, it is advisable that you read more than your child. As you start this habit, you can ask your child to read as little as a few words or a sentence on each page. Naturally, as your child gets more confident, they will start reading more.

You can accompany this activity with the necessary clarifications, and questions to help your child fully access the meaning of the story you are reading together.

Echo reading:

This activity is a modelling exercise where you read a sentence or part of it, and your child repeats. You can start doing this activity when your child is able to decipher quite confidently words without yet being able to read fluently. On top of pointing at the way words are read, the aim is to show your child the intonation of words, how to put a stress on some of them, how to pause according to the punctuation. It helps your child read fluently before they can do it on their own.

When doing this activity, your child should be following with their finger where you are reading, and then point again at the letters/words they are reading while reading. This will help your child focus on the different details (graphemes, punctuation). It will also help you judge whether they are actually paying attention to the details or if they are just repeating (which they should not be doing). Note that if your child can only repeat and not follow along with their fingers, it is a sign that it is still too early for your child to do this activity. Leave it, and come back to it when they will be a more confident reader.

Chorus reading:

Your child and you read at the same time. It is a way for your child to be supported when deciphering the words. This will consolidate their knowledge of the various graphemes and characters.

If you hear that your child is struggling with some graphemes or characters, take the time to remind them. E.g.: "Do you remember? 'e' and 'a' is pronounced [ɛ] as in 'h**ea**d'".

Predictions:

Before starting a new book or chapter, it is a good idea to have a little conversation with your child about what you think is going to happen. You can have a look at the cover together (illustration, title, blurb) to work out what the book is going to be about. If you see characters, you can also ask about their personality. If you are picking up from where you left, remind each other what you read before. Then turn a few pages to have a peek at a few pictures and discuss what could happen next. All these assumptions will give your child guidelines to then confirm or reject them. Understanding the storyline will become much easier.

By modelling this practice, your child will be equipped to do so on their own when they will (start) read(ing) independently in any language.

Inference:

It consists in understanding pieces of information that are not mentioned by using the "clues" the author left in the text. Here is an everyday situation as an example: You arrive home from work around dinner time. Standing outside your house, you see the light on in the kitchen. You can infer that either dinner is being cooked or that everyone is already eating.

This skill can be casually developed using simple questions such as "Have you noticed that ...?" or "Why do you think ...?". Taking the time to point out these details to deepen the understanding of the story will help your child appreciate them even more.

All the activities mentioned in this section can be done as casually or formally as you wish.

Tips to start journaling in a fun way

The more writing practice your child has, the easier it will get. On top of developing writing skills, journaling can be beneficial to children (and adults) on many levels. To name but a few, it helps them become more conscious of their feelings and deal with their emotions; it improves their memory, communication skills and creativity; they can experience various events more fully.

However, the prospect of writing might not be appealing due to the effort it requires. And even if they are more than happy to keep a diary in their strongest language, it might not be the case in all their languages.

When starting, the main aim is to create a habit of regularly reflecting on their daily experiences.

Verbal reflection – *Rose - rose - thorn – bud* [91]:
This is a gratitude game where the participants reflect on events that happened on the day or recently.

For the first rose, each participant mentions the highlight of their day. The second one also invites them to share another highlight. The third round is the "thorn" for everyone to talk about one thing that did not go so well. And the "bud" is for something they look forward to in the future, whether it be near or far.

In this exercise, you will be able to help your child articulate their thoughts and feelings in the home language. Going from there to writing on paper is a small(er) step.

Visual diary:
As the saying goes "A picture is worth a thousand words". If your child is only starting to be able to write short sentences, drawings and photos can be a less

[91] González, Amy. "Game Ideas: Rose-Rose-Thorn-Bud." *Our ml home*, 20 Feb. 2021, ourmlhome.wordpress.com/2021/02/20/game-ideas-rose-rose-thorn-bud/.

intimidating way to start a diary. They can then be annotated with key words and/or have a sentence or two summarising or explaining them.

A variation (or a step-up to this stage) could be that you come up together with one or two sentences. You then write each word on separate pieces of paper and jumble them up. Your child then needs to stick them in the correct order.

Rewriting:

Especially if the home language has a different script from the majority/school language, or if it has a deep orthography[92], it can feel daunting to write. Here is one way you can help your child start writing by modelling it.

Using the idea *#61 Spot the Mistakes*, you can write a few simple sentences to describe your child's day from their perspective and include inaccuracies. Your child will be able to copy most of the text you wrote and change only a few parts. E.g.: It was your child's birthday, and they had a chocolate cake, but you mention that it was a strawberry cheesecake.

Note that in order to read, your child "only" needs to recognise the words. However, when writing, they need to know accurately all the details of each word (spelling, strokes). By providing a text that they can mostly copy, the task is easier as they will only need to remember how to write a few words or sentences. The relatively small effort compared to the amount written will give your child a sense of accomplishment. Rapidly, they will want to add precisions to the text and really make it their own.

Carrying on with the birthday example, you might write "It was such a nice party!". Your child might want to add "It was the best day ever!! My parents are the best!!!". Once they start personalising the sentences you provide them, it will not be long before they can start writing their journals on their own.

The aim is to give them a taste of the emotional state they will be in when they will be able to put all their thoughts on paper, before they can do it. This will help motivate them to carry on this task until they can do it on their own.

---

[92] See glossary at the back for an explanation (p222-226).

Conclusion – How to keep it going

Now that your child has a good grasp of reading and writing, is your job done? Well, not really. Your child probably sees your language(s) is/are interesting, relevant, and "worthy" of dedicating time and effort. They are now more independent and are able to access written material without your help. But remember that without regular practice, your child's skills will rust. It is therefore important to keep the momentum going.

Here are a few ways you could do it:

Reading:

1) Keep on reading with your child every day. Nurture your child's love of reading by creating these bonding moments. As mentioned in the first chapter, you do not have to restrict yourself to only books in the language(s) you are transmitting to your child. Chances are that you have much easier access to books in the community language, and the main goal should be to develop interest in books. However, you can find books that are in your language(s) and will pick your child's curiosity.

2) Change the language on different devices to your home language. It will give your child frequent exposure. And the fact that they need to understand what is written to be able to access the various commands, in addition to the frequent exposure to the words written, will help your child remember them.

3) If you communicate with friends or family in a written way, let your child read and contribute to the conversations (as long as it is something you do not mind your child reading of course!)

Writing:

1) Ask your child to write the list of grocery shopping (and let them add a couple of items of their choice!)

2) Writing a letter, an email, or messages. Big celebrations such as birthdays or Christmas are the perfect time to write nice messages to people we love. You could also help your child write a letter to Santa. If your child loves a book, why not write a letter to the author?

3) There are now, in many languages and countries, companies that send personalised letters to children to which your child can reply. This is a very engaging way to read and write in the home language. Some companies have a character going on adventures, others tell you the beginning of the story and your child needs to say how they want the story to carry on. (A famous French company is Epopia. In the United Kingdom, Unicef uses the Paddington bear character to send personalised postcards to tell your child about the incredible lives of children around the world)

By teaching your child to read and write, you have embarked on an amazing journey that will become a treasure your child will thank you for. Hopefully all the ideas of games and activities included in this book have helped you and will carry on helping you create fun memories with your child(ren) that make the journey as enjoyable as the destination.

Please do take some time, once in a while, to revisit "Chapter 1 – Before Starting". The activities are tools to help your child practise reading and writing in various ways, but this chapter summarises how you should use these tools, and what you need to keep in mind for the experience to be as fruitful and enjoyable as possible.

If you came this far in the book, I hope you enjoyed it and found it useful. Please, do let me know the activities you enjoyed or the part of this book that you found the most helpful, or maybe a note written by your child in your home language? You can email me at contact@library4multilinguals.com

I wish you many more lovely moments spent with your family, reinforcing your ties with your home languages and cultures.

It has been an honour sharing all these ideas with you. For more resources and ideas visit www.library4multilinguals.com and feel free to follow me on Instagram @multilingual_dad.

Glossary

Agreement

Noun-Adjective agreement:

In certain languages such as French and Spanish, the ending of an adjective matches the noun it describes. We say that the adjective "agrees" with the noun it describes.

E.g.: the adjective "black" can be written "noir/ noir<u>e</u>/ noir<u>s</u>/ noir<u>**es**</u>" in French and "negr<u>**o**</u>/ negr<u>**a**</u>/ negr<u>**os**</u>/ negr<u>**as**</u>" in Spanish depending on the noun they describe.

In English, whether you describe one car or two, the adjective "black" stays the same: One black car / Two black cars.

In French, a car (une voiture) is feminine. The mark of the feminine being a final "e", you would translate it by "une voiture noir<u>**e**</u> / deux voitures noir<u>**es**</u>". The "s" marks the plural.

In Spanish, a car is masculine (un coche). The mark of the masculine being "o", you would translate it by "un coche negr<u>**o**</u> / dos coches negr<u>**os**</u>". The "s" marks as well the plural.

Subject-Verb agreement:

Similarly, in some languages such as French and Spanish, the ending of a verb changes according to its subject (i.e. the person/object doing the action).

In English there are only a few traces of it. E.g.: it is necessary to add a "s" at the end of a verb in the third person singular (he/she/it). E.g.: I/you/we/they **sing** – he/she/it **sing<u>s</u>**.

Antonym

An antonym is a word meaning the opposite of another one. An antonym can be a completely different word, like "strong" is the antonym of "weak". It can also be made using a prefix (e.g.: "**im**possible" is the antonym of "possible") or a suffix (e.g.: "care**ful**" is the antonym of "care**less**").

Article

Articles are small words placed before a noun. In English, there are two types of articles: definite (the) and indefinite (a, an).

E.g.: **the** car (definite article); **a** car (indefinite article)

Note that in English, adjectives and adverbs can be placed between the noun and its article. E.g.: a really big car (a = article; really = adverb; big = adjective; car = noun)

Cognate and False friends

In different languages, we can find words that sound and/or look similar. When their meanings are close, they are called **cognates**, and when they are far apart, they are **false friends**.

For example, in English and in French, the word "constipation" points at a condition in which there is difficulty in emptying the bowels. They are therefore **cognates**.

On the other hand, in Spanish, "constipación" is a common cold. "Constipación" and "constipation" are therefore **false friends**.

Grapheme

It is a written symbol that represents a sound. A grapheme can be a single letter or a combination of letters that make up a sound.

For example, the English word "red" is made up of the three graphemes <r> <e> and <d>. "Head" is made up of the three graphemes <h> <ea> and <d>.

Hanzi / Kanji

Both words refer to the Chinese characters. *Hanzi* being the Chinese name, and *kanji* the Japanese one.

Many basic characters are derived from images (E.g.: 火 (fire) 山 (mountain) 川 (river) 田 (field)) They are therefore referred to as *pictograms*. As they represent ideas, they are also called *ideograms*. For example, the characters 動 means "movement / moving" and 物 means "object". Combined, 動物 means "animal".

Each character is formed by different components, also called a **radical**:

動 contains 重(heavy) and 力 (power/strength/effort).

物 contains 牛 (cow) and 勿 (not/negation).

In dictionaries, *hanzi/kanji* are generally grouped by characters that contain similar radicals and by number of strokes. The radicals group the characters by idea. E.g.: 氵 meaning "water" can be found in the following characters 河 (river), 涙 (tear), 酒 (alcohol), 池 (pond), 海 (sea).

Hiragana and *Katakana*

The Japanese language can be written using three different types of characters: *kanji* (see previous entry), ***hiragana***, and ***katakana***. The last two forms are syllabic alphabets. Each character represents a syllable. A word is therefore simply written as it sounds, syllable by syllable.

Using the *hiragana* characters a child can write every word in the Japanese language easily. Later on, they will learn *kanji* that will become especially helpful to differentiate homophones.

Katakana are exclusively used to write foreign words. E.g.: フォーク (fork), ナイフ (knife), スプーン (spoon).

Homophone

Homophones are words that sound the same but have different meaning. (Their spelling can be similar or different).
E.g.: eye / I – flew / flu – hour / our – new / knew – night / knight – flour / flower.

Kinaesthetic learner

"Kinaesthetic" refers to movement. A kinaesthetic learner is a person who learns best when involved physically. Great examples of activities for such learners are field trips, role plays, miming, and any activity that requires movements.

Mnemonic

It is a way to trigger your memory and help you remember things. To remember the order of the planets around the Sun, you can for example remember the sentence "**M**y **V**ery **E**asy **M**ethod **J**ust **S**peeds **U**p **N**aming **P**lanets". By following the order of the words in this sentence and looking at the first letter of each word, it becomes easy to name the planets in order (**M**ercury, **V**enus, **E**arth, **M**ars, **J**upiter, **S**aturn, **U**ranus, **N**eptune, and **P**luto).

Orthography

This word refers to the spelling of words.

Some languages such as Spanish and Korean are described as having a "**shallow orthography**" as words are generally spelled the way they sound. One sound (phoneme) corresponds to one grapheme.

Other languages such as French and English have "**deep orthography**". In other words, one sound can be written in various ways. E.g.: In English, the sound/phoneme [ɛ] can be written in various ways as the following words demonstrate. "r**e**d, h**ea**d, s**ai**d".

Phoneme

A phoneme is the smallest unit of sound that can distinguish two words in one language. E.g.: [b] and [r] are phonemes in English as "bed" and "red" are two different words.

A phoneme can be represented by one or more letters. For example, in English, the word "fresh" contains five letters, but four phonemes [f] [r] [ɛ] and [ʃ].

Prefix, suffix and radical

The **radical** of a word (also called "root") is the smallest unit that bears meaning. Words that contain the same radical are part of one **word family**.

E.g.: The **radical** "dict" (or "dic) has Latin origins and means "to say". It is present in words such as "dictate, dictation, dictator, contradict, benediction, predict". All these words are part of the same **word family**.

A **prefix** and a **suffix** are units that can be attached to a radical - respectively before and after it – to modify its meaning.

E.g.1: the word "predict" contains the prefix "pre-" meaning "before". Therefore, "to <u>pre</u>dict" means <u>to say</u> what is going to happen <u>before</u> it does.

E.g.2: the suffix "-able / -ible" refers to the possibility. "Predict<u>able</u>" describes something that <u>can be</u> predicted.

Register

This refers to the degree of politeness. In some languages, the way you address a person will change depending on your relationship with them.

In French, for example, if you address one person who is a friend, you would use the informal "tu". However, if you want to show respect you would use the formal "vous". Similarly, in Spanish, the "tú" form is used to address someone informally, and "usted" to do so formally.

In languages such as Japanese, there are more levels of politeness. They vary according to the person you address as well as the person you are referring to.

Retrieval process

This refers to the act of accessing information stored in the long-term memory. The more we retrieve a memory, the more we consolidate it[93] and the easier it becomes to remember it. Numerous games and activities in this book provide cues to help your child go back in their memory to retrieve the information. For example, in #28 Hangman, the letters guessed and their location in the word as well as the total number of letters act as cues to remember the word.

Synonym

Synonyms are two words that have a similar meaning. E.g.: "meaningful" and "significant" are synonyms.

[93] Squire LR, Genzel L, Wixted JT, Morris RG. Memory consolidation. *Cold Spring Harb Perspect Biol*. 2015;7(8):a021766. doi: 10.1101/cshperspect.a021766

International Phonetic Alphabet (IPA)

The IPA is a visual way to transcribe sounds / phonemes. In dictionaries, the IPA is used to help the reader know how to pronounce the words.

See below the phonemes mentioned in this book with examples in English and/or an explanation to help you understand how to read them.

VOWELS	
IPA character	**Example / explanation**
[a]	Short "a" sound as in "cat, sad".
[æ]	This is also a short "a" sound, that is pronounced closer to the front of the mouth. In American English, the words "cat" and "sad" are pronounced with this sound.
[ɑ]	"a" sound that is pronounced at the back of the mouth as in "arm" and "calm"
[I]	This is a short "i" sound as in "live, fill, bit".
[i]	This is a "i" sound pronounced with the lips stretched on the side as in "leave, feel, beat".
[o]	This is a "o" sound pronounced with closed lips as in "bored, nought"
[ɒ]	This is an open "o" sound as in "hot, holidays"
[ə]	This a sound produced in the centre of the mouth. E.g.: addition, the.
[e]	This sound is most often found combined with the sound [I] as in "cake" or "layer". In French, it corresponds to the letter "é".
[ɛ]	This represents how the letter "e" sounds in "bed" and "red".
[y]	This is a distinctive French sound represented by the letter "u".

[ɛ̃] [œ̃]	These characters represent nasal vowels typical of the French language.

CONSONANT	
IPA character	**Example / explanation**
[dʒ]	This is how the letters "j" and "g" are pronounced in the words "**j**uice" and "**g**iant".
[j]	This corresponds to the letter "y" in "**y**es" and "**y**ellow".
[ʃ]	This represents how the letters "sh" sound in words such as "fre**sh**, **sh**are, **sh**y"
[X]	This sound can be found in words such as the Jewish celebration "**H**anukkah", the Scottish pronunciation of the famous "Lo**ch** Ness", the Cuban drink "Mo**j**ito", and the Mexican "**J**alapeño pepper".
[f] / [s] / [r] / [l] / [k]	These characters are very transparent and represent respectively the letters "f", "s", "r", "l" and "k/c" in words such as "**F**rance, **S**pain, **R**omania, **L**ithuania, **K**orea".

Can you remember these random facts about languages?

(See: Chapter 1 / *Common teaching mistakes* p21)

Which one(s) of the 5 random facts can you remember without needing prompts? Why do you think? Were they shocking or surprising facts? Can you relate to them more than others? Did you know it/them already? If so, how come you still remembered this random fact?

- Now, here are a few prompts for each fact:

1- Two most translated books.
2- Percentage of daily written words that the 1000 most used words represent.
3- Number of Arabic words in Spanish.
4- Number of words to refer to the rain in Hawaiian.
5- Which language has the longest alphabet? How many characters are there?

⇨ Now reflect.

- Which fact came back to you as soon as you read the prompt?
- Which one did not?
- Why do you think you could / could not remember them?

- Here are the random facts again.

1- The most translated book is the Bible. The second one is *Le Petit Prince* (*The Little Prince*) by Antoine de Saint-Exupéry.
2- Although the average adult knows passively (i.e. understands but does not necessarily use) 40,000 words, 1,000 of them represent 89% of the words used in everyday writing
3- Spanish contains about 4,000 Arabic words.

4- The Hawaiian language counts over 200 words to refer to the rain.
5- Cambodian has the longest alphabet with 74 characters.

- How did you feel about those details you could not remember?
  - Keep in mind that reading again these facts will have reinforced them in your memory.
  - If you could not care less, chances are that in a month time, you will still not remember them.
  - Were you frustrated? Or maybe felt some joy in rediscovering them? All these strong emotions will help you remember these facts.

- How did you feel about the details you could remember?
  - Their significance to you, the fact that you find them incredible, and all the strong feelings will reinforce these facts in your memory.

Test yourself again in a few weeks or a month!

Printed in Great Britain
by Amazon

64615546R00132